Becoming
The Best U

Becoming The Best U

While Watching Your Life Go Down the Drain

The Lessons Cancer Taught Me

Nancy Rugart Plummer & Robert Rugart

Published by Becoming The Best U Publishing

ISBN (paperback): 979-8-9891250-0-5
ISBN (ebook): 979-8-9891250-1-2

Book Cover Design & Front Photo by Kelsie Reimer Fischer
Back Photo (Nancy during cancer) by Laura Turner Photography
Back Photo (Nancy and Robert) by Todd Zimmerman, Pictures by Todd
Book design and production by www.AuthorSuccess.com

Printed in the United States of America

*The information and advice contained in this book are based upon the research and the personal and professional experiences of the author and do not constitute medical advice.

THIS BOOK IS DEDICATED TO MY CHILDREN
WITHOUT WHOM I WOULDN'T BE HERE TODAY

TO MY MEDICAL TEAM
WHOSE HARD WORK AND DEDICATION SAVED MY LIFE

TO MY GRANDSON
WHOSE LAUGHTER REMINDS ME WHY WE'RE HERE

AND TO ALL THOSE THAT HELPED ME ALONG THIS JOURNEY
YOU KNOW WHO YOU ARE

I AM FOREVER GRATEFUL

Contents

Foreword

I first met Nancy in the lounge of our favorite med spa. We would chat and enjoy coffee and pastries, and every week she would introduce me to her newest client. Helping women love themselves has always been part of her calling. She offered structure, support, and opportunity to those who had lost hope of finding the thing they lacked most in life: confidence.

One Saturday, Nancy stopped coming. I was shocked to hear of her diagnosis from a mutual friend. The woman I knew had been fashionable, bubbly, and full of joy. Now she was fighting for her life, undergoing hours of surgery, weeks of recovery, and months of chemotherapy. Despite her poor prognosis, she survived. Shortly after remission she started enjoying life again, only to have her cancer return with a vengeance.

Instead of admitting defeat, Nancy battled on, reinventing herself at every turn and emerging from her experience the best version of herself I have been fortunate to know. She remains the fashionable, bubbly, and joyous person I met at the spa years ago, but now she is also down to earth, infectiously optimistic, and full of the wisdom that only comes from years on the battlefield.

Becoming the Best U is more than a how-to manual or recall of events. It provides inspiration, offers support, and raises the constant possibility of a new perspective and hope to anyone who has been brushed by one of life's many challenges. Nancy's wit, humor, and strength are intertwined throughout the pages of this honest and, at times, raw memoir.

Cancer had no idea who it was dealing with.

Much Love,
Dr. Lori Alfonse
Breast Surgical Oncologist by calling; Nancy's Biggest Fan by heart

An Open Letter to Caregivers

Caregiver is such an interesting word. It carries this tremendous gravitas, like it has to accompany some selfless act of sacrifice, otherwise it hasn't really been earned. I think, however, that we are all caregivers, all the time. All it really entails is wanting and trying to make your loved ones happier, and what is love if not that?

Some of my favorite memories were formed during my stints as "caregiver," from throwing a wig party with my sisters to raise money for medical bills, to playing the piano for a room full of cancer patients, doctors, and nurses to sing along with, to giving my wife an awesome mohawk before shaving off the rest of her hair. Sure, if a loved one is traversing a particularly challenging patch of life, there will be moments that aren't fun. There will be a lot of tedious paperwork, you may need to confront or even replace their medical team, and you will hear the on-hold music of their insurance company in your sleep.

Don't forget, however, that your number one goal is to bring both them and you joy. Take breaks, share your passions with them, and spend some time remembering why you're doing all of this. There's this phrase I love, "Comedy is just tragedy plus time."

If you can, try to spend that time laughing with your loved one. That's what they need most.

Robert Rugart

Introduction

We've all heard the phrase, "When life gives you lemons, make lemonade." I don't think that person had just been told "you have cancer." No one is prepared to hear that news. I certainly wasn't.

Before my diagnosis, I thought I had life all figured out. I was a successful relationship and wellness coach, making six figures, and living a life most people have only dreamed of. I helped hundreds of clients navigate the most treacherous journeys of their lives. Now I had to navigate the most treacherous journey of my own.

It was the summer of 2016, and the words, "Ma'am, you have ovarian cancer," flung me into an odyssey that took me from desperation to determination and forced me to learn the lessons and strategies that we share here. This book is a compilation of my own experiences, insights, and hard lessons learned, plus incredibly creative ideas and sage advice from my caregivers who inspired me throughout my war with ovarian cancer stage 4 and metastatic brain cancer.

We all know someone suffering from cancer, whether a family member, colleague, or friend. It's about time we start sharing the realities of cancer and offer guidance, not just for the warrior, but for their caregivers too. My story isn't about HOW I survived; it's about how becoming Upbeat, Unstoppable, and Unafraid gave me the chance to.

Through heartwarming and hilarious stories, we will hopefully inspire you to see humor and hope even in the midst of despair.

My caregivers were incredible, but I believe my cancer journey propelled them to become better versions of themselves. I hope their contributions inspire all caregivers out there to become the best advocates they can and push boundaries to have challenging discussions with their loved ones and medical team.

I asked my youngest daughter how this experience changed her life, and was so touched by her response that I wanted to share it here with you:

My first experience with ovarian cancer came when I was twenty, designing the play 'WIT' as a theatrical lighting designer. The heart-wrenching script by Margaret Edson shows a woman's life brought to a close by ovarian cancer. They say life imitates art, and a few months later my mother was diagnosed with ovarian cancer.

My siblings and I arrived at the hospital to find my mom, a woman normally svelte and full of zeal confined to her hospital bed, contorted with pain, cancer overwhelming her abdomen. Over the months that followed, people told us to be patient and trust the doctors to do what they do best, but those words of comfort left me feeling helpless. Despite having many patients to attend to, her oncologists made us feel that our mother's cancer was a priority and encouraged me to understand the disease that suppressed her lively self as she began an aggressive course of treatment.

Those experiences were with me as we celebrated her remission the following year, and I was not only overjoyed, but inspired to learn more and do more. In a few years' time I had transitioned my career from the stage to the hospital, now a third year MD student at the Lewis Katz School of Medicine. Experiences with my mother's care led me to concentrate on the importance of communicating with my patients, both early and often, as well as making healthcare a consistent priority despite how healthy someone may seem.

I'm in remission now and am living a fulfilling life. My path has changed many times but I've never trusted my footing more than I do now. Cancer taught me how to pivot. Cancer also taught me humility, resilience, gratitude, and empowerment. It forced me to reach into the depths of myself and find more strength than I thought was there. It was cancer that taught me how to live each day to the fullest.

Don't wait until you're looking death in the face. The lessons I learned from cancer are life lessons for everyone. They're right here in this book.

Just turn the page and start *Becoming the Best U*–Upbeat, Unstoppable, and Unafraid.

I

Are You There Doc? It's Me, Cancer

Our greatest glory is not in never falling,
but in rising every time we fall.

−Confucius

Looking back, my case was like that of so many women now dead and gone. I had felt bloated for months on end. Despite my lack of appetite, when I did try to eat, I had trouble digesting food. I was constantly going to the bathroom to pee, but my constipation could last as long as a week.

I called my gynecologist of twenty-five years and made an emergency appointment two days before Thanksgiving. A superstar in the world of gynecology, I was certain he was the right person to share my worries with. I hadn't told anyone about the visit. As sick as I felt, I was still nervous and embarrassed to see him for fear he would think I was overreacting.

I was dressed for success, having just come from a meeting with a prospective client. We started out with small talk, his asking about my three children whom he helped bring into this world, my asking about his practice, his marriage, his son. My anxiety was growing. "Something is wrong with me; I just know it!" I blurted out.

He looked at me and smiled. "Nancy, look at you. You look beautiful and you've always been a perfect specimen of health."

I stared at him dumbfounded. The voice in my head was screaming, "what does wearing a pretty outfit and makeup have to do with my health?!"

I felt like a little girl being scolded by her teacher after asking to see the nurse. My mind was reeling. Did he know how hard it was to gather the courage to make an appointment? Did he realize how dismissive his words were? Did he not trust my intuition? I was livid. After a heated discussion he begrudgingly agreed to schedule an ultrasound a couple of weeks out. I left his office feeling angry, confused, and humiliated.

I didn't tell anyone about my appointment with my doctor, nor about my upcoming scan. After the test I waited impatiently for my results. I was sure they would have an answer to my pain. They never called. Ten days after the scan I finally called them. My test was clean. The nurse didn't suggest a follow-up appointment and I was too deflated to request one. Despite my unimproved condition, according to my doctor I was officially a healthy woman.

They call ovarian cancer the silent killer; maybe it is just that no one is listening.

I spent the next seven months fighting through discomfort and indigestion. The pain I felt increased so gradually that I was able to adjust and compensate; I kept up with my demanding work schedule, gym routine, and family outings as my symptoms worsened and my condition steadily deteriorated. By the end of June, I could barely force down one meal a day; to make up for lost calories and to self-medicate my unbearable pain I had taken to drinking multiple glasses of wine.

My body had suffered enough, and at the end of a particularly grueling week I knew I could not go on like this any longer.

A friend brought me to the emergency department where the on-call doctor decided to perform a quick ultrasound. Again, it came back clean, and again my doctor tried to discharge me with a clean bill of health. This time I was determined not to let the doctor have the last word. I stared him in the eyes and in as commanding a voice as I could muster, told him "I'm not leaving here until we know what's wrong with me. I think I'm dying and it's your job to save me."

In a calm, respectful voice he replied, "Let's save you then. We'll get you a CT scan right away."

For the first time, it felt like someone was finally listening.

The CT scan showed what the ultrasound could not: a large mass extending from my uterus to the base of my lungs. The doctor did not mince words, I had cancer, and it was bad. When my children heard, they rushed to the hospital, called out from work, started alerting other family members and friends, and became my fiercest advocates, never leaving my side for two weeks.

My incredible gynecologic oncology surgeon gathered a team of eight specialists and scheduled my debulking surgery. He needed time to, in his words, gather the best and brightest, and I needed two procedures beforehand to remove a half gallon of ascites (cancerous fluid) from my abdomen.

For over ten hours I had eight surgeons poking, prodding, and lopping off pieces of me. Have you ever played Operation? It felt like I had one team taking out my funny bone, another on my Adam's apple, and a third on my Charlie horse. I felt emptier than Cavity Sam at the end of a game. (In reality, I underwent exploratory laparotomy, modified radical hysterectomy, bilateral salpingo-oophorectomy, rectosigmoid resection, appendectomy, omentectomy, splenectomy, distal pancreatectomy, right diaphragm stripping, end colostomy, and intraperitoneal port placement.)

My surgery was a success on paper, but all I could focus on was that I would have to poop into a bag attached to my stomach (my ostomy bag), perhaps for the rest of my life. I still recall excruciating agony that no amount of morphine could soothe. It wasn't just the searing pain; it was more the unspeakable truth of my prognosis. It was all too much. *I had cancer.* I just wanted to die.

I almost gave up while recovering from that first operation. I had been thrown into a war that has no winners even if it leaves survivors. I had always heard that the hardest part of cancer was chemo; how was I supposed to make it if I could barely handle my first operation? The pain was unbearable. I felt like a revolver had been emptied into my guts; each of my butchered organs a bullet wound. After hours of lying on a steel slab, every muscle was so sore I could barely turn my head to see my visitors. All I could do was lay in my hospital bed and wait for this nightmare to be over.

One of my first battles was with cachexia, a wasting disease that occurs in up to three quarters of cancer patients and is responsible for almost a third of cancer-related deaths. Before I went into the hospital, I was considered slim. While recovering from my first operation I lost over twenty precious pounds in just a few weeks. It wasn't that I didn't want to eat, it's that my body felt like it couldn't. As one who has rarely been comfortable with food, I have delved into the emotional and physical thin edges I walk on in order to eat healthily. This time was different.

Cachexia impacts a cancer patient's mental health as well, and it certainly did mine. As the pounds kept falling off my family begged me to see my regular psychologist. After our meeting he prescribed antidepressants. My medication allowed me a brighter outlook, giving me a better chance at fighting my cancer.

It wasn't enough to get me to eat, however. My cachexia had taken over. While I was being released from the hospital, my children were given the crucial task of getting me to gain back the weight I had lost so I could start chemo. Their attempts to beg and barter were futile. They knew they had to try something more radical.

My children reached out to their network and procured some edibles. I still remember that day, lying on a recliner in the heat of the summer, turning down any bit of food, my children begging me once more to try just a morsel. I tried to refuse, still terrified what it might do to my ostomy, but at their insistence I took a tiny bite. Little did I know that said morsel was, in fact, a cannabis infused gummy bear.

Before I knew it, I was begging for more food. My children gathered around me, plying me with baked goods, certain they had their answer. Gummies worked not just to stimulate my appetite, but to dispel my fear of having my ostomy explode after eating. I never looked back.

Over the next few weeks, I slowly returned to an acceptable weight. With chemotherapy back on the table, I had to come to terms with the next step of my journey. It terrified me. I didn't believe my body could handle chemo after what it had endured. This cancer journey had already been too much for me. My kids begged and begged, and finally I realized I had to at least give it a try.

My chemo regimen was as challenging as I feared. With each new day I was dealing with another side effect—infection, nausea, dehydration, exhaustion. Each time I returned to the hospital I faced more setbacks. The toll each session took added up; every day of chemo was my worst day yet. My ostomy made it worse. Many long, lonely nights I laid on my bathroom floor, too tired to lift myself off the ground after cleaning up a disgusting mess from my ostomy, only for it to explode again.

It went on like this for days, weeks, months. America celebrated its birthday, schools opened, Thanksgiving turkey was carved, Christmas presents were opened, the New Year brought fireworks and the hope of a new beginning. Two weeks later I was pronounced "in remission." I rang the bell, jumped for joy, and congratulatory toasts were made. To my chagrin, I felt numb and increasingly powerless as more and more people heard the news. I realized they thought of cancer as merely a win-lose situation. As they celebrated victory, the reality of my situation began to sink in.

When my war with cancer began, I had an army to rival Hannibal and his elephants. From my medical team to family, friends, and kind strangers, this army had given me immeasurable help in beating cancer. Now that I was in remission the calls had stopped and, outside of routine checkups, my medical team had disbanded.

My family and friends were exhausted beyond belief, and they too needed to move on with their lives. Cancer had almost destroyed me and every part of my life. Now it was up to me, and only me, to pick up the shards and try to piece them back together.

The prevailing thought is if you are lucky enough to get to remission, then you have won. Your war is over. Time to put down your weapons, call yourself the victor, and send your troops home. Time to get back to life as normal. Normal? What was normal? I had no idea what to do next. I lay in my bed each night, too embarrassed to tell anyone how scared I really was.

I was certain my cancer would come back, and soon. I couldn't picture a life longer than a few months; perhaps, if lucky, a few years. Statistics said as much. Less than half of women survive five years after their ovarian cancer diagnosis. I was so convinced my cancer would return I kept shaving my hair for almost a year into remission so I would not have to endure the trauma of losing it again.

Before I was diagnosed, I had a thriving business, and while almost half of my clients stayed (partly, I suspect, to be supportive) I could barely muster enough energy to serve them. My business had been as a life coach, helping men and women feel empowered with the dating world and other relationships. Now my own relationship with my husband of four years was on shaky ground.

My husband, bless his soul, had been unable to cope from the moment of my diagnosis. It was not that he didn't love me or that he didn't care. He truly could not handle even the thought of cancer, let alone the realities of it all. The man who had been so romantic before couldn't kiss me or even approach my hospital bed. We were never the same after that.

Although outwardly he was wonderful, inside he withdrew. While trying to save my own life, I was secretly trying to save our marriage as well. I lied to the world and told everyone how supportive he was and that we were doing great; all the while I was immensely lonely and heartbroken by his emotional absence. I felt abandoned. I watched our marriage slowly fade away. We separated and filed for divorce just months after my remission. I finally had my health, but no longer had a home.

My father and I fought our cancers side by side. Days before separating from my husband, my father lost his battle. I felt numb, unable to express my despair and sadness. My losses from cancer had been greater than I could stand. I couldn't even cry at his funeral.

The next day, I tried to commit suicide. Thankfully I did not succeed, yet despite being in the care of compassionate psychiatrists, nurses, and caseworkers, I was unable to accept the help they offered. For five days I sat despondent, just waiting to be discharged.

I hit my lowest point that final day. My soon to be ex-husband had promised to pick me up from the hospital. Instead, he chose to drown his feelings at a local bar. I knew then that nothing remained of my former life. I had a choice, to rise from its ashes or to sink into them until swallowed whole. I realized we had all fought too hard for me to give up now. I couldn't disrespect the sacrifices my army had made to get me this far.

As one who had overcome depression before, I knew I had to make real changes. I needed to heal from the trauma I had endured. I had to start focusing on myself and find out what I now wanted out of life.

I asked myself, "What have I learned from this journey? What if I took the lessons I learned and applied them to my life every day?"

I learned that I need to accept the things I cannot change and change what I can.

I need to ask for help even when healthy.

I need to get my affairs in order.

I need to push myself.

I need to take life one step at a time.

I need to be willing to adapt and develop new strategies.

I need to accept that grief is the price we pay for love.

How to start incorporating these lessons? I had always known that surroundings have a huge impact on quality of life. I needed a fresh start. Warm weather was what my frail body craved. Knowing one of my dearest friends (who had been an incredible advocate of mine through this ordeal) was ready to welcome me with open arms in Miami, I packed up and started my new life in November 2017. I started growing my hair back the day I arrived.

Eight months later, while vacationing in Rome with a friend, I collapsed from a grand mal seizure and was whisked away by ambulance to the nearest public hospital. I regained consciousness sixteen hours later, six other patients and I crowding their ICU, all wearing diapers and hospital gowns, IV lines draped over us like spider webs.

There was no air conditioning, no fancy equipment. No one spoke English. I wasn't told what had happened nor why I was there. I sat shell-shocked and panic-stricken. It was another four hours before the neurologist came in and told me (in English) that I had a brain tumor and would need to undergo more MRIs and CT scans before brain surgery.

My youngest daughter flew out to Rome to help coordinate my transfer of care to a surgical team in Miami. After nine long days of tests, I was flown back to the U.S. for surgery. Metastatic brain cancer was my prognosis. This is what I had feared. Emaciated, half my hair shaved off, and separated from reinforcements by several state lines, I was worried that my emotions would take over. Life had reverted to that never-ending war, fighting the same old fight just in a different arena. This time, however, I had the tactics I had gleaned from my previous battles.

I just had to remember them and put them into practice. Instead of suffering silently, I reached out to my old battalion and new acquaintances. Since I was still new to town, my local army was just a few friends who had busy lives of their own. My daughters flew to Miami to see me through my brain surgery. Thankfully the surgeon was able to remove the tumor almost entirely. I was aware however of my new cognitive and physical challenges. Words did not come easily, my balance was shaky, but I knew to push myself and take things one step at a time.

Two months later an MRI revealed the brain tumor had grown back and I would need radiation surgery. Over the next several weeks

I asked colleagues to come help and a few of my closest friends took turns flying to Miami to come stay with me and help me through my convalescence. More strategies were developed. My affairs were in order.

One month later I was declared in remission again.

Cancer almost won. I survived what my medical team had thought was an impossibility. I'm a miracle they say. I learned recently at a survivor's support group that the median lifespan after brain metastasis of ovarian cancer is five months. I'm still here, five years after having a part of my brain removed, and seven years after first hearing the words "you have cancer."

I'm past worrying that it will come back. Instead, I'm forever grateful every morning that I'm not just alive, but living my life to the fullest. Even though I have to deal with an exhausted body that was ravaged by cancer, surgery, chemo, radiation, and seizures, I'm healthy enough to encourage others to advocate for themselves, gather the courage to change the things that they can, and always focus on the positive.

Is my cancer journey over? Of course not. Even though, thank goodness, I'm in remission, I'm dealing with the scars from my battles. My body was reconstructed so my digestive system is always at odds. I still have to search for words that my brain just can't find. I've had a few mini-seizures so I've had to pivot and adjust to life without a car. My journey with cancer hasn't been an uphill battle; it's been a roller coaster fraught with terror, trials, and triumphs along the way.

So many times I thought I was starting to get my life back to normal only to have the rug pulled out from under me. So many endless nights too anxious to sleep for fear of having another seizure. So many times feeling depressed from this endless war.

Yet, when I put the lessons I learned with cancer to work every moment of every day, repeat my mantras, "accept the things I cannot change and change what I can; ask for help even when healthy; get my affairs in order; push myself; take life one step at a time; pack a toolbox of strategies; and accept that grief is the price we pay for love," I'm much more grateful, empowered, and prepared for what more will come my way.

I still stumble. I still fall. But as Confucius so wisely stated, "Our greatest glory is not in never falling, but in rising every time we fall."

Reflections for the Warrior

- ◆ I learned that I know my own body best. Pay attention to how you feel right now, starting with your head and working your way down to your toes. What feels off? List some things you could ask your medical team about today. Worst case, you understand your body better for the future, best case you save your life!

  1.

  2.

  3.

- ◆ I learned the gravity of losing too much weight while having cancer. Cachexia is a serious disease and affects as many as three quarters of advanced cancer patients. If you start losing a lot of weight, please don't ignore it. It could cost you your life. Talk to your medical team. Cachexia is poorly understood in the medical field so you may find yourself having to self-advocate. Most importantly, find a way to stimulate your appetite. Keep a journal of your weight below so you have a record to show your doctors at your next visit.

DATE   WEIGHT

_____

_____

_____

_____

_____

- If you're feeling depressed, anxious, or overwhelmed, please take this seriously and share honestly with a confidante or your medical team. Don't be embarrassed or upset with yourself. Life can be hard and overwhelming. Psychologists and psychiatrists can play a crucial role during your cancer journey, either for yourself or your family. Patients and caregivers often deal with anxiety, depression, mood swings, and cognitive changes even after remission.

Don't put your mental health off for one more day. Write down a confidante or medical team you will reach out to today and discuss your feelings. Please be open to receiving psychiatric or counseling help to get you through whatever you're dealing with. Please, if you're feeling really alone or having any thoughts of suicide, call or text the Suicide and Crisis Lifeline now at 988. They're always here for you 24/7.

Musings of a Caregiver

Every person at some point in their lives has been or will be a patient. If there was one thing I could tell everyone, it's that you know your body best! While you might not understand why you feel the way you do, you know when something isn't your normal. You shouldn't be embarrassed or scared to tell your care provider what you're feeling, and equally as important: what normal means for you.

A medical team is there to support you—to combine their knowledge with your input to make the best diagnosis and provide whatever the best care is for you. When my mom's medication made her drowsy, but it was prescribed to be taken with breakfast, she worked with her team and found a way to get the same benefit without the impact to her daily life, she just had to ask. Unless it is a dire emergency, you are an autonomous decision maker and can always ask for more time to make a healthcare decision or more information and input before doing so.

It's your body to go home and thrive in, so speak up and take on your role on the team: you are the leader!

-Paulina Rugart

One of the most important things we as caregivers can do is pay attention to our warriors. Take the time to have an open and honest conversation with them about how they're feeling, both physically and mentally, but also perform your own evaluation. Yes, their medical team should be gathering this information too, but they are busy with a million other things and details might get lost in the shuffle.

You may have to advocate for them if you think the advent of a new symptom or worsening of an old one merits further investigation. I wish we'd been able to advocate for my mom when she first went to her doctor, but she hid her symptoms from us too well. Later in her treatments, we made sure her doctors knew what side effects she was experiencing and worked with them to minimize their impact on her life. Remember, your warrior is already fighting a war with their own body; they probably don't have the energy to fight one with their doctors too.

Speaking of having the energy to fight, it's incredibly important that your warrior keeps their weight up. Often the thought of food can make patients queasy, or they may be too tired to eat anything. Do what you must to feed them. For my mom, harnessing the munchies was incredibly helpful, but maybe your loved one can't say no to a good milkshake or onion rings. If nothing seems to whet their appetite, lemon sorbet was always in high demand around the hospital floor when I visited. Don't worry too much about nutritional content; gaining a few pounds is far preferable to losing all of them.

Fighting through cancer is an incredibly depressing experience, and many people contemplate suicide as an "easy" alternative to surgery, chemo, and recovery. You may have to have a frank discussion with your warrior about their mental health. Seriously contemplate involving professional help if you think you or your loved one may be depressed. There is no shame in being unable to handle some things on your own.

–Robert Rugart

Reflections for a Caregiver

* It's scary watching loved ones lose a precipitous amount of weight. As a caregiver, one of the greatest gifts you can give your warrior is to make sure they keep eating. Talk with your warrior about what food they're comfortable with right now; for us, onion rings and lemon sorbet worked wonders.

* Often as a caregiver it can be easy to prioritize your warrior's mental health over your own. Write a sentence or two describing how you're feeling today. Don't be embarrassed or upset with yourself if you're feeling depressed, anxious, or overwhelmed. It's normal.

_____

_____

_____

_____

* You can't help your warrior if you're overwhelmed with challenges yourself. Be sure to develop a self-care routine to relax and reduce stress. This could include taking a walk in the park, watching your favorite TV show, reading a book, or anything else you might do to wind down. If you need help, don't be afraid to ask for it from another member of your army or a trained professional. There are a number of support groups available to caregivers online and through most hospitals. Please, if you're feeling alone or having any thoughts of suicide, call or text the Suicide and Crisis Lifeline now at **988**. They're always here for you 24/7.

2

How Did You Get a Piano in Here?

God, grant me the serenity to accept the things I cannot change,
the courage to change the things I can,
and the wisdom to know the difference.
- REINHOLD NIEBUHR

People always assume I must have been this great fighter from the start; that when I heard the words "cancer" I was undeterred and ready to go to war. That's as far from the truth as possible. When I awoke from my first operation and was told of my condition, I shut out the world. I couldn't accept my prognosis, my pain, or my fears. I gave up.

My fighting spirit had been crushed over the previous seven months of doctors dismissing my symptoms and my condition deteriorating. My husband's lack of support and my body's laundry list of failures didn't help either. I sat in the hospital numb, not caring that I was wasting away. I watched my life slowly falling into the abyss with each passing day. Where I had always loved biking, hiking, and enjoying the outdoors, my life from that point and going forward would be mostly in a bed or chemo chair with stale air and a sterile atmosphere, pooping into a bag and living life more for the destination than the journey.

What was it that helped me choose to fight? What was it that my doctors and loved ones said, in their kindest, albeit stern, caring ways? Although they might not have known it, it was the serenity prayer. You don't have to be religious or a member of Alcoholics Anonymous to appreciate it. Reinhold Niebuhr is recognized more as a philosopher, ethicist, and author than as a preacher. His words are powerful. They became my mantra.

First, I desperately needed to accept the things I could not change. I could not change the fact that I had cancer, my business had been halted indefinitely, I had no income for the foreseeable future, and I was too weak to stand on my own. Every minute I was thinking of dying and not fighting for my life, my chances of surviving were getting slimmer.

Thankfully my army showed me compassion, helped me with my morose perspective, and reminded me that despite my dire situation *there were things I could change* within the confines of this new life. **That in every moment, one pivot might make all the difference.**

My army had modeled courage to change the things you can on day one. To start, my son became a legend at the hospital overnight. While waiting for my team of surgeons to be assembled, my son and his father (who deserves so much credit for his love and support) bought an electric piano from a nearby music store. They promptly marched it through the doors of the hospital with such confidence that, although they received a few odd glances, no one questioned their movements.

I don't remember much from that first stint in the hospital while waiting for surgery, but I do remember the music. Drifting in and out of consciousness, loved ones surrounded me while my son and others took turns playing my favorite tunes, and everyone, including some doctors and nurses, joined in to sing. They sounded like angels. Still to this day, whenever I'm feeling down, I relive those memories.

Little by little I saw how small changes could impact my cancer journey for the better. The suffocating feeling of stale hospital air was easily fixed with a few potted plants. The monotonous drone of life support machines couldn't hold up to the music of a few lively friends. The flimsy, chilly hospital blankets were quickly replaced with cozy, comforting fleece. Every minor improvement made me feel more human; made survival seem less a dream and more a reality. Despite all the things I couldn't change in my life, taking control of the parts I could made me feel upbeat for the first time since this hellish journey began.

Now I had to deal with my hair falling out from chemo.

I've had friends call me sobbing after losing their first clump of hair. I had cried with them, feeling so powerless. I was determined not to let cancer win this time. I planned a **"Shear Luck Party"** with my daughters and a dear friend for the day after my first chemo session, and deliberately shaved off all my hair at once. Rather than letting cancer dictate the timing, I found it quite empowering to choose when and how I would lose my hair. I felt I was in control; a feeling that was rare considering my circumstances. I arranged for my niece, a professional photographer, to do a photoshoot the next day to commemorate my new look. Sometimes it's important to rip the Band-Aid off.

Think about it . . . what if you took charge and determined *when* you would lose your hair? **Change the things you can.** It won't make the reality of it go away but it might make you feel more in control. I've had clients and friends who took my advice and they actually felt relieved to get it over with, rather than anxiously waiting for clumps to fall out. When I later attended a friend's **"Shear Luck Party"** we all took turns with the scissors and razor, stopping to appreciate a few different hairdos along the way. Everyone's favorite was the mohawk, and I think that was when our warrior started to feel like she could really handle this.

Months of chemo still lay ahead. My daughter held my hand as she read my schedule. Every week for six straight months I'd have to sit in a chair for five hours while my body was pumped full of poisons that would hopefully kill the cancer before it, or they, killed me. I refused to be one of those women wearing a ratty t-shirt and baggy sweatpants while struggling to knit a scarf that would never be worn.

Fortunately, my daughter had a wonderful idea. What if, instead of dreading the days of chemo, we celebrated them? **Turn Chemo into Chem-whoa! Make chemo days about celebrating life!** Every Wednesday we would rifle through my wardrobe for stylish tops, sleek skirts, and stunning jewelry. After a few weeks, we saw other women joining in. Our nurses started looking forward to what we'd wear next and, instead of being a day fraught with fear and anxiety, chemo became the day that I looked forward to every week.

Some fears, however, were harder to conquer. My ostomy was my nemesis. It took me forever to have the courage to see it as the lifesaving tool it was. Pooping in a bag sounds messy enough, but it doesn't begin to describe the disgusting issues that come with it. Don't believe the pamphlets, in reality you have a cheap, antiquated vinyl bag glued to your stomach that falls off, leaks, and generally makes a total mess of anything you dare to bring near it. Best case scenario, you constantly smell faintly of feces. Worst case scenario, the contents of your intestines explode out and stain clothing, upholstery, and carpets while drenching every other surface around you. Despite its downsides, I now realize I never could have survived without it. Healthy people take their sphincters for granted but I can promise I never will.

I'm so grateful to my children and those that invented creative ways to add fun moments to my war with cancer. Whether bringing a piano into the hospital, dressing up for my chemo visits each week, or going out for a manicure or a movie afterwards, my army courageously broke the mold, and it changed my cancer journey completely. Every pivot was a win, and every win was another milestone in my journey to overcoming cancer.

When coaching my clients, it's been fulfilling to help them figure out what they can change in difficult situations. A few months ago, one of my clients had to be put on insulin and called me to share. She felt the same way I did with my ostomy; unable to see insulin as a life-saving tool. We spoke for hours, letting her air her frustrations and worries about how giving herself insulin shots and checking her levels was going to wreak havoc with her normal lifestyle. Together we realized that, while she couldn't change her newfound need for insulin, we could change her schedule to better accommodate it.

Slowly but surely, she calmed down, and with trepidation she began her new regime. With more coaxing and cheerleading from me and her family, she finally accepted insulin as the lifesaving tool that it is, resulting in less anguish and more energy to spend with her new grandson.

Experiences like these are why many recite the Prayer of Serenity so often. Life isn't for the faint of heart. Every day we are thrown curveballs, some harder to hit than others. Remember these words of wisdom so many have found comfort in: Grant me the serenity to accept the things I cannot change, the courage to change the things I can, and the wisdom to know the difference.

Reflections for the Warrior

- I learned it takes serenity to accept the things I cannot change about my situation. Write a few obstacles *you cannot* change in your life right now.

    1.

    2.

    3.

- I learned it takes courage to change the things I can. Write a list of things *you can* change about your circumstances.

    1.

    2.

    3.

- I learned that one pivot can make a difference in your life. List one pivot or small change you can make today to help improve your emotional, mental, or physical well-being.

_____

_____

_____

_____

Remember, just one idea can make a difference!

Musings of a Caregiver

My mom absolutely HATES being told she can't do something. She's always been a go-getter, and is happy to put in the extra effort to have things her way. So, when cancer struck and she really had to accept that she couldn't change her situation, she sank into a very dark place.

Fortunately, my sisters and I quickly set about improving her situation, changing the things we could. The first step was to distract her from her circumstances and make sure she felt loved. We snuck a piano into her room, but you know your talents and warrior better than I do. Something as simple as reading them a book or reminiscing together will let them know how much you care.

Next, we tried to make her feel more comfortable and at home. Pillows and blankets were switched out for easy to wash, but much fluffier, versions of the stock hospital wares. We brought in plants, flowers, and greenery to disguise the sanitized appearance of her room. With every change her mood visibly improved.

It can be incredibly difficult to accept that which you cannot change. By instead focusing on the things you CAN change, you show your warrior just how much control they have over their situation. And, if your warrior is anything like mine, that might be the difference between staying down for the count and getting up to fight the next round.

-Robert Rugart

Reflections for a Caregiver

- As a caregiver it can be difficult to accept what your loved one cannot change. Write a few obstacles that, despite your best efforts, cannot be changed in their life right now.

- As a caregiver we all have special talents, whether cooking, playing an instrument, or planning an uplifting event. Write a few things that you could improve about your loved one's circumstances.

    1.

    2.

    3.

- As a caregiver remember you need to put on your own oxygen mask before assisting those around you. List one pivot or small change you can make today to help improve your own emotional, mental, or physical well-being.

_____

_____

_____

_____

3

Hey, I Know We Haven't Talked in a Few Decades, But...

When you don't ask, you don't get.

—Gandhi

Cancer crashed into my life like a tsunami. My hopes, my dreams, and literally everything about my daily life washed away. Working, gardening, entertaining, hiking, traveling, making love—all were gone in a moment. I went from having a fabulous, fun life where I could support others to a life where I needed help just to get out of bed.

I needed much more help than I could ever imagine. I needed help emptying my Foley bag, since another of my chemo side effects was my body couldn't urinate on its own. I needed help taking my medications. I needed help deciphering what the doctors and nurses were saying. I needed help eating and drinking. I needed help negotiating with the insurance company. I needed help getting to chemo and twice-weekly infusions. I needed help dressing, bathing, getting back into bed. I needed help with everything.

No one wants to admit they need help. I certainly didn't. However, I became brazenly aware that I was going to die if I didn't start accepting it. Unfortunately, my husband at the time was not able to do much more than work longer hours since my business was put on hold.

Who was going to take me to my chemo appointments? Who was going to help me when I landed back in the hospital again? Who was going to take me to my specialists' appointments? Who was going to make our meals? And what about getting my medications? I quickly realized how many people I would need to survive my cancer journey with the fewest possible battle wounds and minimal PTSD.

I realized that just accepting assistance wouldn't be enough. I needed to check my humility and **ASK FOR HELP.**

I knew what I had to do. I was totally powerless on my own. Too weak even to stand by myself, too sick to be able to speak for more than a sentence or two, too scared to be able to hear what the doctors were saying, I leaned into my powerlessness.

I realized what I needed was an army. I also realized I had absolutely no idea how to build an army. I was desperate. How many people are even in an army? I knew it wasn't one (despite the phrase), but maybe it was two? Or five? A hundred? Either way I knew it would just be me unless I started recruiting people one at a time.

I started with my family, but many people find their army through the American Cancer Society, which offers tremendous programs and services such as a 24/7 Cancer Helpline, a navigation support to help figure out the next steps, plus potential financial resources. In addition, your medical team should have support groups in your area and be able to point you towards additional services you may not even know exist.

Another great resource is Caring Bridge, a nonprofit whose vision is "a world where no one goes through a health journey alone." They report that over 300,000 people use their site every day to offer love and support. Their website offers a GoFundMe page, MealTrain to organize food preparation and delivery, and much more.

The first recruit was my youngest, tech-savvy daughter. I relinquished my phone and let her manage all the texts, emails, and calls that erupted after word got out. She didn't keep it for one day or one week; she kept my phone for a whole month, and gracefully asked everyone to resist the urge to visit, which didn't always go so well. She went a step further, maintaining a blog on PostHope to keep caring friends and clients updated. The amount of support and outreach I received from this was overwhelming. If I have one piece of advice for you, it's to be honest about your experience on social media; you'll be amazed at how many people want to help.

My son took on the role of physical trainer. When I had pneumonia, my doctors prescribed a spirometer to develop my lung capacity. He cajoled, enticed, and berated me to practice. Had he not refused to accept my excuses it would have sat on my bedside table and collected dust. Without my spirometer, I may have died even before my chemo treatment started. Once my breathing was under control, he took it a step further by encouraging me to start walking, stretching, and even biking.

Since I was at high risk for infections, visitors were rarely allowed the first few times I returned home. My children continued to play the piano, sing my favorite songs, and watch movies with me. I insisted on watching movies like *Schindler's List*, *Life is Beautiful*, and *The Fault in Our Stars*. My kids quickly put their foot down. From here on out we would only watch upbeat comedies. When friends and family returned for movie nights, I wasn't allowed a vote. This proved to be a wise choice.

My eldest daughter stepped up and offered to rearrange her schedule at law school so she could take me to my weekly chemo treatments. Somehow, she also found time to research ovarian cancer treatments to better advocate for me. On the days she couldn't make chemo for tests or presentations, she encouraged me to reach out and ask friends to fill her shoes.

I did. Remember, I was desperate. I called a childhood friend who lived in New York, asking her if she would mind taking my daughter's place every so often. "Of course," she responded, but thought it odd since we had barely talked in years. I don't even know why I thought of her, but I believe it was meant to be. She told me months after my remission she was so shocked to hear from me that she asked her mother for advice. When she called, her mother replied, "Of course you will be there. It's divinely inspired." She took her new role and ran with it.

Our friendship flourished. She was incredibly helpful again and again, coming to my aid at times when others weren't available. She not only came through whenever my daughter couldn't take me to chemo, but was also able to help my other daughter who was studying in New York City. Since then, she and I get together often, and I now consider her one of my besties.

Many people have told me that their children live too far away or that their network is too tiny to ask for help. What they don't realize is how many connections they've made throughout their life. I had to resort to requesting help from a friend who lives three hours away whom I hadn't spoken to in decades. Hopefully, you can find the strength to do the same. Your life depends on it.

I was a shadow of myself, unable to drive to doctors' appointments, grocery stores, pharmacies. I could hardly stand, let alone cook or clean. With my chemo brain, I could barely decipher my medications or instructions, let alone handle my health insurance company. A friend sat with me and helped plan a course of action enlisting the aid of as many people as possible. She enumerated the tasks I required help with and who might be best suited to each mission. When I protested, she looked at me and wagged her finger, as if to say, what else are you going to do? She was right. I was desperate, and to survive my cancer, my army wasn't big enough. I was going to have to recruit more soldiers.

I asked a friend to join me and my daughter and learn how to self-catheterize, since she used to sell them to pharmaceutical companies. I asked my brother and his wife, a nurse, to drive 600 miles to join me for my treatment plan appointment. I asked neighbors to help take out the trash. I asked one of my brothers to sneak his puppy into my hospital room. At the time I may have felt I requested too much, but I left my ego at the door, and everyone involved has since told me they enjoyed playing hero for the day.

I remember while I was stuck in the hospital in Rome, under observation after my grand mal seizure, unable to sleep from all the medications my doctors plied me with, one of my dearest friends in Miami FaceTiming me (to avoid roaming charges) to listen to my drug-induced hallucinations. She brought humor to what would otherwise have been a fearful situation. I'd describe my bizarre nightmares and we just laughed and laughed at the absurdity of it all. Her time and attention were the greatest gift I could hope for.

When people ask my advice on how they can best help a friend who's dealing with cancer, I often share this story and suggest they just be available to listen and, if possible, bring laughter.

Winning my war with cancer did require an army. So, what's my advice?

Every good army needs some generals. While you will have to be the five-star general in your campaign, your family, loved ones, and doctors will serve as your three- and four-stars. It's your job to pick the right team to make healthcare and life decisions for you. While almost all of my doctors were incredible, I had to fire one because he seemed more interested in his research than in my outcome. You need to know that your army is making decisions with your best interests in mind.

To start, ask the doctor who discovered your cancer to help you find an oncologist. Request a referral but be ready to do your own research. Choosing your medical team can take time and you may even want a second opinion. You'll want a doctor that specializes in your type of cancer and one that participates in your insurance plan including Medicare and Medicaid. Every day we hear about new therapies to fight cancer.

Each cancer needs different treatments, so don't just assume that chemo or radiation is going to be the best one. From proton therapy to immunotherapy and new surgical options, new treatments are being offered every day. Do your research; even better, enlist your army to help figure out the best plan for you. Moreover, make sure your doctor has the training, education, and patient reviews that give you the confidence you need.

Bring someone to your appointments to help you decipher any new information. Who should you ask? Someone you trust that will have the guts to ask challenging questions and hear tough news. Make sure this person is reliable and organized.

This can be a challenging task when you're feeling vulnerable. Don't be afraid to ask tough questions yourself. Can you meet with the team beforehand? At which hospital do they practice and on which days? When you do meet with the team, make sure you're comfortable with the doctors, nurses, and staff. Do they have someone on call when the doctor is away? Is it easy to make an appointment? What is their treatment plan?

If anything is worrying you, please take the time to get a second opinion. Don't be embarrassed. Getting a second opinion is very common. Let your doctor know you'll be asking elsewhere in order to better understand your situation. This new doctor may not agree with the first finding or treatment plan. If you're still not satisfied, keep searching until you feel safe and ready to go to battle.

As you begin treatment, expect your doctor to keep you informed throughout each stage of your journey. Don't be shy about calling and asking questions even when you think you should know the answer. They can't help you unless they hear from you. Every cancer battle is different and every day new issues will arise. **Advocate for yourself! Speak up! Ask for help again and again!**

While it's so important to keep asking for help, it's also so important to be grateful; a simple word of thanks means a lot. Be courteous and compassionate when your wait time for an appointment is longer than normal. When I was a patient in Miami, the care was extraordinary but the wait times were abominable. Often, I arrived to meet with one of my specialists and saw the chalkboard sign displaying a wait time of over two hours. I always brought a book to read just in case. I realized the doctor was often delayed by other patients in my exact situation. I have so much compassion for the doctors I saw trying to comfort parents, siblings, and extended families. Thank them again and again. They deserve a medal of bravery every day.

Cancer has humbled me in more ways than I care to remember. I am forever grateful for the help I received. I made it a point to express my gratitude to everyone I could, both seen and unseen. I thanked nurses, doctors, janitors, phlebotomists, pharmacists. I made huge posters for my oncologist team with lottery tickets attached as a holiday card. I brought plants to the receptionists. I wrote thank you notes to friends and family.

Yet, there were also too many people I never thanked enough. All the meals dropped off, the countless cards, texts, and calls of encouragement, and I never got a chance to thank them in person. There were so many people, from receptionists, MRI technicians, coffee baristas, friends, and family, that gave of themselves to help me during my low moments.

Now it's your turn. Put on your general's uniform. Start recruiting. Write your list and make specific requests for help. Start asking and don't stop asking even after you've gone into remission. Please don't be afraid. I know it can be hard to ask for help, especially when you're in such a vulnerable place.

Not everyone will say yes. In fact, I've advised my clients to expect a no, so when they get a yes, they'll be pleasantly surprised. Moreover, some will say yes and not show up. I've spoken to far too many cancer patients whose experience with trying to gather an army was devastating. Families abandoned them, friends fell off the phone chain, and some created a hostile situation.

You might never know why people go AWOL. I implore you not to take it personally when people don't show up for you; as hard as it is to accept, it isn't about you. We never truly know what's going on with someone's psyche even when they appear to want to be helpful. Many people are terrified of the word cancer, let alone the realities. Some get scared because cancer reminds them of their own fragility.

I can certainly attest to the devastation of having a loved one not show up. It feels like a huge betrayal. Two friends of mine created such a hostile environment that I had to ask them to leave my home and never come back.

However, my life depended upon finding help. My cancer was positively debilitating. Thankfully, since I asked and begged dozens upon dozens of people (even strangers), I got enough help to get me through the next day. And the next. I became unstoppable.

I finally came to peace with those that couldn't show up for me during my cancer journey by focusing instead on the heroes that did. I instinctively knew that the energy I was wasting staying angry was just hurting me.

I truly threw away my ego to survive. I needed to get help to win this war with cancer. And as Mahatma Gandhi once wisely taught us, "If you don't ask, you don't get."

Reflections for the Warrior

- I learned I needed an army to survive my war. Write a list of groups from which you can enlist your army (family, friends, church, Facebook, cancer support groups, Rotary, gym, neighbors, etc.)

    1.

    2.

    3.

- I learned I occasionally need to ask for help whether I'm sick or healthy. Write a list of the things you need help with, big or small, and who might be the best person to do it. If you're struggling to come up with a person to help, maybe you can come up with someone who knows that person instead.

    1.

    2.

    3.

- I learned that people love to be helpful and that one bit of help might make all the difference. Pick one thing from the list you really need assistance with and reach out for help today.

_____

_____

_____

_____

Remember, just one idea can make a difference!

Musings of a Caregiver

Every time I've been a caregiver, I left the experience feeling as if I could have done more. I used to be ashamed of that, but I have since realized that the two options were to feel like I did too little or to feel like I did too much (with, I suppose, some tiny third possibility of having perfectly nailed what ends up being a very quickly moving target.)

It's essential as caregivers not to end up in that latter camp. If you've ever flown on an airplane, you'll recognize the line "put your own mask on first before assisting others." Remember, at the end of the day, the most important person to take care of is yourself. Burnout is a very real phenomenon; this job is a marathon and you need to pace yourself to make it to the finish line.

Fortunately, caregiving is a task that can be handled by multiple people! I think that's what we did best when taking care of my mom—instead of one person helping her 24/7, she had an army of people taking care of her a few hours at a time! I've seen many other caregivers try to handle everything themselves, presumably because they were confident they were the best person for every job and couldn't trust anyone else with their loved one. Check your pride at the door and let your army divide and conquer!

–Robert Rugart

Reflections for a Caregiver

- As a caregiver, it can be easy to take on too large a burden and risk burnout. Who can you call on to help share the load?

    1.

    2.

    3.

- When dealing with a challenge it is often hard to focus on anything else. What are some things your loved one doesn't realize they need help with, and how can you or another member of their army provide assistance? Examples may include taking their dog for a walk, dropping off groceries, or picking up their children from school.

    1.

    2.

    3.

- Every burden off your loved one's plate can help them deal with their current challenge. What is one thing you could do right now that would make their life easier?

———————————————————————————

———————————————————————————

———————————————————————————

———————————————————————————

4

Where There's a Will, There's a Way

The art of living well and the art of dying well are one.

—Epicurus

My youngest daughter looked at me with trepidation. "Mom," she said, "you're overdue on your phone, insurance, and credit card bills. What do you want me to do about it?"

My darling nineteen-year-old was sitting with me on my hospital bed. It had been over a month and I still hadn't been home for longer than a couple days. While I was fighting for my life the bills were piling up. I couldn't care less about my financial problems. Thankfully, she could.

Once again, she proved herself an amazingly wise advocate. I handed over my passwords and she took care of the rest. (Please don't be overwhelmed if you don't have a financially-prudent daughter available to help you out. Call someone in your army who is savvy with money and has the patience of a saint.)

That was only the beginning. It's embarrassing to share my naivete when it came to my financial health. I truly had never thought much about healthcare insurance, retirement savings, disability insurance, social security benefits, Medicaid and Medicare requirements, wills, or advanced directives. I was in for a crash course.

My first wake-up call was learning what wasn't covered by my health insurance. Luckily for me, I had good medical coverage and had paid my premiums (thanks to my daughter)! Sadly, however, our nation's healthcare system doesn't help patients and their families with the realities of these tough situations. Even if you have the most expensive plan, there are so many medical expenses that are out-of-pocket. For instance, if you have to self-catheterize, like I did, most insurance companies will only pay for four catheters per day.

Please tell me who pees exactly four times per day, especially after hours of chemo each week? And wigs? The best insurance will provide two, which, if you wear them each day like I did, will get ruined in just a few weeks. Heck, one of my best friends had her wig catch fire while she was getting a casserole out of the oven!

So, what did my children do? They broke the mold again. Instead of panicking, my daughters threw me a **"Wig Party"** while I was in my third stint at the hospital. Friends, family members, and clients all came out to show their support. My daughters had borrowed some wigs from a salon for everyone to vote on and donate to our cause. It was basically a fundraiser where people bought tickets to support their favorite look. I was supposed to be at the party trying out each wig, however, plans went awry and I was stuck in the hospital.

Pivoting yet again, my wonderful children helped me video chat into the party. I was grateful to connect with so many loved ones and get a chance to thank each one for their support. With the money raised, I bought the two wigs that received the most votes and wore them proudly, smiling sweetly each time I wore one at the fond memory of such a joyous celebration. Through the generosity of my army, the donations were used not just to buy wigs, but enough medical supplies to get me through the tough days to come.

Next, I had to deal with the insurance company. I was too stressed from my day-to-day struggles and suffering from "chemo brain" to make much sense of all the bills, co-payments, and medications, so my darling daughter took on the challenge. My first recommendation is to make sure your premiums are always paid on time, otherwise they can cancel your health insurance.

Second, don't pay any bill until you have the final Explanation of Benefits. Call your insurance company and whoever sent you the bill as many times as needed to understand any discrepancies. If you are using employer provided insurance, check with your benefits manager, as many offer programs to help navigate these issues.

Don't be afraid to try to negotiate bills or be put on a payment plan. Just recently I called my hospital to discuss my last bill for the year. They informed me if I could pay in the next two days, I would receive a 20 percent discount.

The National Cancer Institute and the American Cancer Society's websites have additional information and resources to help those with or without health insurance. Their studies have shown that cancer patients working with community healthcare workers (CHW) had more home care and fewer emergency and hospital visits.

Please don't give up. Call the American Cancer Society for resources. Depending on the type of cancer you have, call support groups both national and local. Work your social media for help and ask your army to do the same.

It can take hours and hours, plus heaps of patience, to sort through the insurance claims and stay on top of your healthcare bills. Accept assistance from your friends and family members who are willing to make life easier for you.

Although I needed to focus on my health, it was necessary for me to examine my financial wellness, too. Questions were spinning around my head. How was I going to fare if my cancer left me unable to work again? Could I get disability insurance? Should I have had life insurance? If I lived to be sixty-five, was I eligible for Medicare? What were my social security benefits if I never worked again?

Until now I had never considered my financial health. I was always optimistic about the future. Cancer was giving me another reality check. Don't wait until you're sick or faced with a difficult situation to plan for your future. I called my financial advisor and pleaded for help. She provided the answers to all my questions and I made the necessary changes to my lifestyle.

Without her help I would have lost precious time and energy fretting over financial battles rather than fighting for my health. Think of meeting with a financial advisor like your yearly checkup; people who don't see their doctor are the ones most likely to receive bad news. Don't let that be you.

Cancer and life's other challenges are harsh reminders to get our affairs in order. Whether you're eighteen or eighty-one it makes sense to have a written will and advanced health plan. Having an advanced care plan that explicitly lays out your intentions will make any difficult times a little less stressful.

You'll want to appoint someone who understands your values and is comfortable being your healthcare power of attorney when you can't speak for yourself. Most health care providers have advanced health care plans preprinted for you to fill out and sign. Review them in detail and don't be afraid to ask any questions before making your decisions.

This also might be a good time to sit quietly with yourself and ask, "How do I want to be remembered?"

Whether you have days, months, or decades, you can choose to spend each remaining moment with grace and gratitude. Perhaps now is the time to let loved ones know how much they matter and rekindle old friendships. Whether through Facebook, text, or phone call, take this opportunity to reach out to someone you haven't made time for and spread a little love.

When the pandemic began, my dear sister organized a weekly Zoom call for us siblings. It was the first time we'd all been together since my niece's wedding. We've continued this tradition even after the pandemic. It's been so heartening hearing about their everyday lives and being able to celebrate milestones, especially with my brothers who live far away.

Want to leave a memento after you're gone? It can be very simple. Whether through words, letters, videos, gifts, or other creative media, you can offer a lasting memory to show them how much they were loved. Don't think about it too much. Just do something. People tend to put things off for another day. Remember, you may not get one.

Planning how your body is handled after death is a question for you to answer while you're here on Earth rather than forcing your grieving loved ones to decide. Do you wish to be buried, cremated, or give your body to science? There are eco-friendly options available if that interests you. Choose the type of service or memorial you wish to have and how you are going to pay for it. Talk to an expert if you have questions.

One of my clients knew her bone cancer was winning the war. She diligently got all her affairs in order in preparation as she continued to fight. She wrote down every last wish, from songs to be sung to types of flowers to casket colors. She found it immeasurably cathartic sensing that her children would feel more peace not having to question what to do with her remains and estate.

Don't procrastinate on these important decisions. Discuss plans with your loved ones. Nothing is more divisive than arguing over an inheritance or funeral plans. Rather than adding stress to an already trying time, provide an opportunity for joy and celebration. It's your life, how would *you* like to be remembered?

Reflections for the Warrior

- I learned I needed to get my affairs in order. Write a list of steps you can take to improve your financial health and develop safety nets for when life throws you curveballs.

    1.

    2.

    3.

- I learned I needed to prepare a will and inform others how I would like my remains and funeral to be handled. Write down what you want to be done with your body and a few specifics you'd like at your remembrance.

    1.

    2.

    3.

- I learned it's important to let my loved ones know how much they matter. Write down one loved one you will reach out to today.

_____

_____

_____

_____

Remember, just one idea can make a difference!

Musings of a Caregiver

They say nothing in life is certain but death and taxes, which makes how little we talk about both so strange to me. Over your warrior's journey, it will be important to discuss and plan for both.

Many people are reticent to discuss their finances, but if your warrior is going to survive this war and live a wonderful life after, they'll have to come clean and be honest about theirs. When trying to coax information out of my mom, she was much more willing to open when I shared my side of things first. No one wants to beat cancer and then have to fight a new war with the debt that comes with it, so try to get ahead of the ball now.

Similarly important is discussing end of life plans, not just in case your warrior dies, but also to help them overcome their fear and plan for their future! Planning for death is really just laying out what is important to your warrior now: who should end up in their will, what they should be remembered for, and how they want their loved ones to feel when they pass. My mom, for example, wants to be cremated and have her ashes spread in her favorite place, the ocean. For her remembrance she would like us to throw another wonderful wig party in her honor, and hopes through it we can continue to carry on her message. Planning a celebration of life rather than a mourning of death will help them feel content about their past, and hopefully optimistic about their future.

–Robert Rugart

Reflections for a Caregiver

- Financial issues are a touchy subject for many people. Depending on your warrior, try to find ways to help them manage their finances that they will be comfortable with. Some may be comfortable with your drawing up a budget, others may be happy for you to organize a fundraiser, while still others may only want you to help find them cost effective alternatives. Honestly evaluate how you can be most helpful to them right now, and realize that sometimes you will need to have uncomfortable discussions if they are going to make it through this challenge.

_____

_____

_____

_____

- End of life plans are something everyone should discuss. Talk with your loved one about what you would like at your own funeral. Maybe your conversation will inspire them. Write down a couple of ideas that the two of you came up with.

    1.

    2.

    3.

• It can be difficult to reach out to people when going through a challenge. Who in your life is going through something and could use a friendly message?

_____

_____

_____

_____

5

Four Letter Word, "Something You See on a Dock"

The goal is not to be better than the other man,
but your previous self.
–The Dalai Lama

I was finally home. I collapsed onto my bed, propped up by pillows, draped in a duvet, friends and family bringing food and drink when I needed them. It was good to be back. In the distance, I heard a familiar voice. Groggily I opened my eyes to see an old friend entering the room. It had been years since we'd seen each other, but as soon as he heard of my condition, he knew he had to visit.

Naively, I expected him to dote on me like everyone else. I was wrong. "Listen," he said, "I came here to look you in the eye and give you some advice. No one is going to do this for you. Chemo is meant to destroy the cancer, but if you don't get up and get moving, it will destroy you, too. You need to start pushing yourself every moment you can. Whoever is strongest, chemo or you, will go on to win this horrific war."

I remembered hearing a little of this lecture from my daughters when I didn't feel like eating another bite or from my son when I didn't want to practice breathing into the spirometer. I took a deep breath and tried not to tear up. This was not what I was expecting from his visit. He continued, "You might think I'm being harsh, but I've seen too many friends die from cancer. I'm not saying you still won't die, but you've got to try harder."

Tears started flowing. This was tough to hear. I felt once again like I was letting my army down. "How am I ever going to do this?" I asked as I lay in my bed.

He smiled and said, "You've got this Nancy. Push yourself every moment because no one else is going to do it for you."

I started with isometric exercises, focusing on one muscle at a time. Lift one leg for ten seconds, relax for five, and repeat. Sounds easy? It felt like I was lifting a log, not my leg. To strengthen my lower back, I'd lie down and curl into a ball for thirty seconds. I got creative with my workouts. This proved invaluable each time I was sent back to the hospital since I was always tethered to the bed with heart rate monitors and IVs.

I constantly pushed myself. I started doing laundry, which involved going down one flight of stairs. I couldn't walk, but I *could* sit with the laundry basket on my lap and shimmy down one step at a time. Once I was proficient with the stairs I graduated to walking around my neighborhood. I requested more help from my army, who encouraged me to bike the mile into town.

The first time we set out I fell off my bike in less than thirty seconds. My friends panicked, running to me and demanding we go back. I shook my head no, brushed myself off, and got back on. My friend's advice had really inspired me. Was "inspired" the right word? I think a better word was "haunted." I kept hearing my friend's warning that chemo would kill either the cancer or me, whichever was weaker. I had to be stronger.

I fell nine times that first day just biking into town. I never gave up. I didn't get hurt. I started repeating the old adage, "What doesn't kill you makes you stronger." When I finally sat down to breakfast at one of our favorite restaurants, I was smiling ear to ear. I had accomplished a great feat. I continued with these minor victories, yet Sundays were always the worst days as my chemo had taken full effect by then. I'd have to be content with my isometric workout or visiting a museum via wheelchair. I listened to my body. I never pushed myself when I felt it would do more harm than good.

I remember one time when I was back to working on a limited basis, I was scheduled to give a coaching seminar on a Sunday. It happened to be very close to home, so I was determined to drive myself. Like all Sundays while receiving chemo, my body was in so much discomfort it was hard to walk, let alone talk.

Resolute, I drove to the community center an hour early, not to have time for setting up, but for crawling up the three steps (yes, three steps, not three flights) to the classroom where I would instruct my students. The exertion was so fierce my ostomy exploded, luckily only once. After crawling and cleaning my mess, I arrived at the room and settled myself just in time for my seminar to begin. For the next two hours I could barely contain my joy. I smiled all the way home.

Exercise was a vital component of my treatment plan and many of my doctors believe it's one of the major reasons I survived. Even in remission, my mantra is "keep moving." Exercise doesn't need to be a daily grind of jogging three miles or taking spin classes. If you can and want to, congratulations. If that's not your style, you can just move your body throughout the day.

What can you do to get your body moving? It doesn't matter what you've done in the past. Begin today. Just push yourself to start with stretches or try doing a few household chores. If you're in better shape, turn it into a social experience so you look forward to it.

Depending on your budget, physical limitations, and time allowance, come up with a list of activities you've enjoyed in the past or may be up for trying now. Invite a friend, spouse, or family member to join you.

A budget-friendly option is a walk in the neighborhood or scenic park. Perhaps you'd also enjoy doing a free yoga or fitness class online. If you work better with a routine, focus on finding a fitness class that you can attend regularly. If you can't or don't want to ask someone to join you, consider a Peloton bike or any interactive home workout equipment. It's amazing how social online workouts can be nowadays. Whatever activities you decide to try, just have fun and be sure to listen to your body.

It was vital for me to push myself physically, but I knew I needed to push myself mentally, too. My brain had atrophied from all the anesthesia during my first round of surgeries. Add six months straight of chemo and you can only imagine how scrambled my brain had become. As most cancer patients will attest, even reading a newspaper article can be challenging.

When I rang the bell, declaring to the world I was "in remission," I vowed to work hard to restore my comprehension. I didn't know where to begin. I felt vulnerable and humiliated until a dear friend of mine figured out how to challenge me in a fun way. She declared one day we were going to do crossword puzzles. I was silently panicking. I was bad at crossword puzzles before cancer. Did she have any idea how hard it would be for me now? I tried to beg off, but she stubbornly launched into reading me the first clue. "Four-letter word, *something you see on a dock.*"

"Duck," I answered, smiling confidently.

My friend couldn't stifle her laugh (we still giggle about it now). She remarked kindly, "Probably not the answer, but it'll get easier."

She was right. We finished the crossword puzzle together and while my head was throbbing, my heart was hopeful. Before she left, I downloaded a crossword puzzle app. I still do a few clues every night before bed when my brain is most tired in order to push myself a little more.

While I was being wheeled into the OR for brain surgery, my doctor explained I may end up with speech impairment or partial paralysis on my right side. When I came to, I started doing my isometrics, focusing on the right side of my body. I squeezed my right hand shut, then my right eye, then tried to lift my right leg, my right arm. I let out an audible sigh of relief. I called the nurse to my side.

Although just at a whisper, I was speaking. I didn't hear any impairment. It was nearly midnight and she told me I was one of her two patients, but the other was fast asleep. I begged her to talk with me all night. I needed to convince myself I was going to be okay. She happily obliged. I had such a sweet conversation with her, learning about her past and hearing about her goals for the future. She kept asking if I wanted to rest. I couldn't. I knew if I pushed myself to keep talking, I could continue to push through whatever issues would come up. There were many.

I was released from the hospital, my memory addled, my speech slurred, and my sentences stilted. One month later my roommate from college flew down to take me to my neurologist appointment and hear the results of my MRI. The day before my appointment, she asked me if I thought my brain tumor was back. I nodded slowly and she took my hand knowingly. We both knew what the MRI would show. I went in for another surgery, this time with radiation to destroy the tumor. It was a success, yet still my comprehension was slow, my ability with numbers was limited, and my recall was greatly hampered.

I believe physical exercise was paramount in helping repair my cognitive faculties. In fact, three days after my first brain surgery, my neurologist gave me permission to fly to DC and attend a wedding. Since the median life span after being diagnosed with metastatic brain cancer from ovarian cancer was under six months, his attitude was "get out there and live!" I called a friend and she agreed to meet me at the airport and be my caregiver. The first day we took a short walk around her neighborhood. I felt exhausted, disoriented, and confused. Each day we added a little more distance.

Five days later we decided to take a nearby hike. Unfortunately, the trail markers were worn and we got lost, causing us to have to climb a few boulders to find our way back. It was exhilarating! In just one week I'd gone from immobile and unaware to agile and astute. I am forever grateful to my friend for pushing me to new heights both physically and mentally. Since then, we've hiked many miles together across the U.S., still getting lost and pushing on with a childlike sense of adventure.

All of my loved ones have been remarkably patient, providing the words I cannot find and happily filling in the gaps of my memories. My synapses are firing a little faster every day. I've been reading more thanks to my book club and the audiobooks I listen to while taking walks. Thanks to my children's suggestions, I've added Sudoku and math brain teasers to my daily routine.

When I first started writing my column and this book, my children took turns editing and talking through what I was trying to say. After reading the first draft of this chapter, my son remarked on how much my writing had improved since we started. Cancer has brought much chaos and destruction to my life, but moments like these remind me that all my effort has been worth it.

Many of my clients are fortunate to have avoided cancer so far, but life's other challenges have still knocked them off their path. One asked me for help getting back into running. She felt her sense of determination had dwindled from all the trauma she endured during her contentious divorce. She knew she'd have to push herself to achieve some of her goals. She was ready. As her cheerleader, I was ready too.

Since she'd been a solid runner before, she felt optimistic about her goal to get back into running. She gave herself seven months to be able to train for a marathon. Every week she pushed herself a little more, feeling more upbeat as her training mileage increased. I kept reminding her to listen to her body and not push too hard if it didn't feel right. She listened. When she got sick or her body didn't feel strong one week, she'd be kind to herself and ease back her running, then push herself a little harder the next week. At the end of the year, she was unstoppable; not only had she run one marathon, but two. Looking back, she said, she realized that her success was in listening to her body and being kind to herself when her body needed a little rest.

She evolved into a great coach for herself to achieve other goals as well, remaining unafraid as she tackled other life's challenges.

Whatever you're doing right now, vow to do more. Try out some apps like Sudoku, or other brain boosters. Ask your friends and loved ones for suggestions. Have fun and look forward to the possibilities. As George Bernard Shaw once said,

Life isn't about finding yourself.
It's about creating yourself.

Reflections for the Warrior

- I learned I needed to push myself physically every moment, because no one else was going to do it for me. Write a list of the ways you can push yourself physically in order to heal or enjoy a healthier lifestyle.

    1.

    2.

    3.

- I learned I needed to push myself mentally every moment, because no one else was going to do it for me. Write a list of the ways you can push yourself mentally in order to heal or enjoy a more fulfilling lifestyle.

    1.

    2.

    3.

- I learned it didn't matter what shape I was currently in. I could change my trajectory for the better with one leg lift. Write down one thing that you can do today to push yourself and move your body a little more.

_____

_____

_____

_____

Remember, just one idea can make a difference!

Musings of a Caregiver

Never underestimate the power of a good cheerleader. With a little bit of encouragement, we all become capable of things we previously thought impossible. A few days ago while rock climbing, my mom got scared on a route and fell off the wall. But when I came over to watch and cheer her on, she climbed straight to the top with no problem!

I feel like many of her challenges during cancer were similar—she was totally capable of handling them, she just needed a push (sometimes a shove) in the right direction.

It's important to have a good sense of how healthy your warrior is on any particular day; their strength the day after chemo may not be the same as their strength a week later. Tailor the challenges you throw at them with that in mind. I know I always demanded more from my mom than she thought herself capable of, but sometimes she was right and I had to lower my expectations for the session. These setbacks will happen, just keep being optimistic and believing in your warrior and they'll start to believe too!

–Robert Rugart

Reflections for a Caregiver

- It can be tough to motivate yourself when going through a challenge. What are some activities your warrior loves that will help get them active and moving? It doesn't have to be athletic, something as simple as walking around the block still counts.

    1.

    2.

    3.

- Cooperative games and puzzles can be a great way to keep your warrior's mind active. What are some activities you could do together that would help sharpen their wits?

    1.

    2.

    3.

- There's no better time than the present. Make plans with your warrior today for one of the activities you listed above.

_____

_____

_____

_____

6

Is Cirque du Soleil
Accepting Applications?

Courage is more exhilarating than fear and in the long run it is easier.
We do not have to become heroes overnight. Just a step at a time,
meeting each thing that comes up, seeing it is not as dreadful as it
appeared, discovering we have the strength to stare it down.
—Eleanor Roosevelt

My nephrologist and oncologist entered the room, heads bent low. Five days before, I had been whisked to the hospital, suffering from severe dehydration and agonizing abdominal pain after my first round of chemo.

When they finally looked at me, I could tell the news was bad. "Your kidneys are failing," they said, almost in unison.

These doctors were my four-star generals and I trusted them to save my life, no matter how dire the situation. I had survived a ten-hour surgery, nineteen days in the hospital post-surgery, and regained the amount of weight I needed to be ready for chemo. I thought once I started my regimen, I'd have a good fighting chance. I never expected it to kill me after just one treatment.

Thankfully, my eldest daughter had stayed the night with me, sensing my extreme anxiety. She lay curled up in my hospital bed trying to give me strength and encouragement. She listened intently while the doctors explained the ramifications and the treatment options. What I needed besides medication was forty-eight hours of non-stop IV fluids and blood work to check on my progress.

My anxiety was escalating. I couldn't sleep, so terrified my body was giving up. I started panicking about my whole ordeal; kidney failure, not being able to urinate on my own, and infections from my ostomy. How was I going to survive this horrible cancer? Had all these battles been worth it? In between sobs, I told her I had given up. No more chemo. I couldn't take it anymore.

My daughter looked at me compassionately and said, "One step at a time, Mom. Let's get your kidneys working first, okay? Then we'll figure out the next step."

I took a few deep breaths. She went on to say, "Mom, you can do this. The fact that you survived your surgery is incredible. If you could live through all that, you can get healthy now and live through chemo. Let's focus on fixing your kidneys and get you home."

I relaxed a little. I guess I was putting the cart before the horse a bit. I didn't need to be a hero today. I needed the strength to tackle my kidney failure head-on. "One step at a time," I whispered again and again to myself.

My creatinine and magnesium levels stabilized over the next forty-eight hours. I was overwhelmed with relief, realizing it wasn't as dreadful as it appeared. Now I had to get strong enough to leave the hospital. I dealt with that head-on as well, taking walks around the nurses' station, eating, and getting more sleep. Finally, after eight days of recovery, I could go home. I had spent twenty-seven of the last forty-three days in the hospital and was scheduled for another surgery in two weeks to switch from an intraperitoneal port to a single lumen port.

That procedure went so well that the morning after I biked with friends into town, my foley bag full of urine hooked over my handle-bars. I hadn't been able to urinate on my own since my first surgery, so my doctors had inserted a catheter with a collection bag the size of a large soup carton. When we got to the outdoor café, the bag dropped onto the sidewalk and burst, causing urine to splash all over.

I broke into tears, humiliated and devastated that I had had to endure so many embarrassing moments only a couple of weeks into my cancer journey. I hadn't wanted to leave the house for fear of this. My daughter looked into my eyes, then took me into her arms for a huge hug. "Mom, look around. Nobody cares."

She was right. At first strangers gawked, but seeing me emaciated, pale, and sporting a wig, they turned back to what they were doing with compassionate acceptance.

My daughter whispered to me, "Remember this moment, Mom. This is why you're doing okay. You're getting out of the house and living life despite your cancer. Someday in the future you'll be able to laugh at this."

I didn't believe it then, but she was right.

After that fiasco I was determined to get rid of my Foley, which I did the next week. I met with a highly recommended urologist. Getting rid of the Foley was simple, however, the next step proved a surprising challenge. My daughter and my dear friend, who used to sell catheters professionally, came with me to the urologist appointment to provide support. My doctor was impressed to see me in something other than pajamas despite my situation and even more thrilled that my army was there to help. "You've got the right attitude," he said with a smile. "Once you start self-catheterizing, you'll feel a whole new sense of freedom. And I'm glad you brought your assistants."

If you're unfamiliar with what a self-catheter does or how they're used don't worry, I was too. It sounds simpler than it actually is. The concept is amazing; a life-saving tool for people who develop nerve damage, disease, or other complications and suddenly find themselves unable to urinate on their own. It allows you to empty your bladder by inserting a thin tube into your urethra and draining the urine into a container or toilet. Here's the hard part. Finding the urethra. Even the pamphlets give one pause. First, you need to gather supplies. Supplies? To pee? A mirror, maybe two. Lubricating jelly, soap, and finally the catheter. I was beginning to realize why he called them assistants.

Laugh if you want because the three of us howled. Imagine a three-ring circus. My daughter on the floor of the office with not one, but two huge mirrors, while I'm squatting on a chair (none of the bathrooms would fit us all) and my friend reading the directions while handing me cleanser, lubricating jelly, and getting ready to hand my daughter a container for me to pee in. I'm not the modest type but never in my life had I felt the need to inspect my urethra, nor had I realized how hard it was to locate.

The pamphlets suggest you put one leg up on a toilet or lie on your back in a frog position, which we found even more hilarious. We decided on the squatting method so there could be one step I was confident in. Laughing our pants off didn't help, but it took us almost thirty minutes to figure out this self-catheterizing business. Our success was celebrated by the whole office—doctor and nurses— coming back into the room as we all giggled some more. Another life lesson: bring in your reinforcements when you're in over your head; teamwork really does make the dream work.

Of course, self-catheters weren't the miracles I wish they were.

Insurance didn't pay for as many as I needed and I had a lot of UTIs as a result. However, they allowed me to return to a more normal lifestyle, and for that I am grateful. Urinating on my own was just one more step in my journey; one more obstacle I'd found the strength to stare down.

With my kidneys back in working order I could finally start chemo again. It was two days after Labor Day and, unbeknownst to us, the busiest chemo day of the year, with people recently returned from vacation ready to face the music. Early that morning we had a fashion show, chose our favorite outfits, and accessorized, determined to make today a **Chem-Whoa** day! We arrived at 9 a.m. sharp and waited our turn. Looking around the room we realized we'd be waiting a long time.

Five hours later my chemo treatment began. We never complained as we felt sorry for the staff. It was a zoo, but we still managed to have fun. The nurses loved our positive vibes and looks, as did fellow patients. We had a great mother-daughter day, and we got a chance to chat about her life. She was starting to date a wonderful man who she later married, and I was lucky to spend my hours learning about their relationship.

The next week my white blood count was too low for treatment, which added another week to my chemo regimen. More tears flowed. I felt this hellish journey was never going to end. However, with the help of my army 1 was learning how to adjust. I'd **pause**, get **perspective**, and **pivot**; I'd reassess my goals and start over again. If I was too nauseous to eat one day, I could make up for it the next. If I hadn't gone biking or walking around the neighborhood that morning, I could still do it in the afternoon.

So many of us have this notion that resetting only happens when making New Year's resolutions. Cancer had taught me that I needed to reset many times, even in the course of a week, in order to survive. I reset all the time now. If my goal is to do a yoga class once a week and

I miss one, I'll try to do two the following week. If I don't get eight hours of sleep one day, I'll try to make up for it the next. I don't let my bad habits—mentally, physically, financially, or emotionally—get a stranglehold on me. It's too important not to. It's much easier to check in with myself a couple of times each day so I can pivot and get myself back on track to a healthy way of life.

Resetting is easier than you may think. It just takes practice. Give it a try now. Is there anything you're doing or not doing that's impeding your goals? Perhaps you're not getting enough sleep, drinking enough water, making time to meet up with friends. No worries. Reset. What do you need to start or stop doing?

Become your own coach. Make the necessary changes starting *now.* Not tomorrow, not next week, not next year. *Now.* Make a phone call or send a text, do ten pushups right now or if that's too hard, start with one. You'll be amazed how much better you feel for doing something small to change your life. **If you need help getting or staying healthy physically, mentally, financially, or emotionally, reach out to experts in those fields.**

Most cancer centers have resources for cancer patients and care-givers, yet many of my caregiver clients came to me asking for help as a cheerleader while they challenged themselves to get fit. They needed even more reinforcement than the cancer center programs could provide. One particular client and I would take walks and talk, or go for a long hike in the park, her 10,000-step goal achieved most days. The fresh air, exercise, and hoorays she got from me slowly gave her the confidence to take her new healthy lifestyle into her own hands. Today, she's maintaining her 10,000 steps per day routine and feeling refreshed instead of depressed while caring for her elderly parent.

Remember, you don't have to become a hero overnight. Just one step at a time.

Reflections for the Warrior

- I learned I needed to isolate my problems rather than paying attention to all of them at once. Write a list of some obstacles that are giving you fear or anxiety.

  1.

  2.

  3.

- I learned I could reset at any time, not just on milestones and holidays. What's one thing you've been putting off because the "timing wasn't right?"

  _____

  _____

  _____

  _____

- I learned that tackling one problem at a time got me further towards my goals than just touching on multiple problems. What is one obstacle you can tackle today?

  _____

  _____

  _____

  _____

Remember, just one idea can make a difference!

Musings of a Caregiver

Sometimes life comes at us fast. There will be times when you or your loved one are overwhelmed with everything that's happening, especially immediately after a diagnosis or procedure. In these moments, I like to use **Pause; Perspective; Pivot** to tackle the problem.

First things first, you need to **pause** and slow things down. With my mom, I made sure she stopped moving, centered herself, and took a few deep breaths to clear her mind, but any method that feels like you are pausing life for a few moments will do. We found that doing this with another person forces you to pay attention to them and helps clear your mind of other thoughts.

Next, you'll want to take **perspective** of your situation. Have an honest conversation about what the future entails. In my experience, most of the time my mother had a nebulous feeling of dread, but she was too scared to actually inspect that feeling and find out what it really was. Often, you'll realize that your future is much more manageable than you thought!

Finally, choose one small **pivot** you can take to improve that future. Maybe your warrior is feeling lethargic and adding a little activity to their day is just what they need! Or maybe they aren't sleeping well and you need to get them a more comfortable pillow or blanket. Maybe it's something more serious and they need to start making end of life plans. Whatever it is, the only way to help them move forward is by taking life one step at a time.

–Robert Rugart

Reflections for A Caregiver

- It's important to be able to **Pause** when you may otherwise be caught up in the chaos of life. What works for you? Maybe it's listening to a relaxing piece of music, or playing with a puppy, or just slowing down and taking deep breaths. Try some things and write down what you thought was effective.

_____

_____

_____

_____

- Take **Perspective** of your situation. What are the most important issues facing you or your warrior?

    1.

    2.

    3.

- Now **Pivot**. Choose one of the issues you listed above and decide on an action you can take to improve it. There's no time like the present; if you can, tackle it today!

_____

_____

_____

_____

7

Can I Wear Lingerie Over My Diaper?

Do not wait; the time will never be 'just right.' Start where you stand, work with whatever tools you may have at your command, and better tools will be found as you go along.

−George Herbert

My experience with cancer has taught me that I need to pack a toolbox with many strategies and mindsets for life. Here are some of my essentials:

SENSE OF HUMOR

The nurse wheeling me to my operation regaled me and my friend with stories of her sister, Mary, who had ovarian cancer like me. She told us about Mary's children, husband, career, home life, and aspirations. I was so happy for her sister that I asked the obvious question as we arrived at the OR door, "How's Mary doing now?"

She answered matter-of-factly, "She's dead, sadly. Died last month."

She then turned on her heels and left us alone for another nurse to retrieve me.

Luckily my friend and I had been through a lot together. We gave each other a knowing look that said, "Really? She tells you her sister died of the same cancer you have just before you go in for a procedure?"

To our surprise we both started laughing uncontrollably. When we finally caught our breath, my friend roared, "You just can't make it up! Who does that??!!"

The next nurse opened the doors to find the two of us still giggling and laughing hysterically. "What's so funny?" she asked.

"Nothing," we responded.

But it wasn't nothing. Humor was the only tool we had that could get us through that moment. If we hadn't laughed, we would have cried. **As the saying goes, laughter is the best medicine!**

PERSPECTIVE

I learned the hard way, however, that it doesn't matter how many tools I have if I don't have the right perspective. **Depending on your perspective, you can view many situations as either positive or negative.** *It's your choice.* Words matter. They change thoughts and feelings. How often do you complain? How often are you grateful? Pay attention. I know it's not as easy as I'm making it out to be. But, like everything else, it gets easier with practice. Cancer taught me how to be upbeat, unstoppable, and unafraid by changing my perspective.

Every night before I go to bed, I name everything I'm grateful for that day, and I mean everything! The more I practice it, the happier

I feel, and the better perspective I have when things go awry. I've had many clients try it and they say it's worked for them. Give it a try now.

SLEEP

When I reach into my toolbox, the next item for dealing with life's challenges is a pillow. Experts have discovered many sleep benefits including increases in immunity, metabolism, information retention, and mood.

Nowadays I strive to get eight to nine hours of sleep each night. Personally, sleep is a non-negotiable. If I don't get adequate sleep, I feel the negative consequences immediately both physically and emotionally. I used to need a two-to-three-hour siesta every afternoon. It's only recently that I can go a full day without lying down. I listen to my body. The life lesson cancer taught me is to allow myself to take naps and sleep more. I can't take chances since I recognize my frailty, so if I'm exhausted during the day, I change my plans accordingly.

Do what it takes to get yourself adequate sleep. A few tips include setting a sleep schedule, avoiding consuming food, alcohol, and caffeine before bed, being active during the day, and removing electronics such as your phone, computer, and TV from your bedroom. Lastly, try to create a peaceful environment where you sleep. Keep it uncluttered, at a comfortable temperature, and make sure it's quiet and dark at bedtime. **Get yourself a pillow and mattress that you truly love—it's not worth skimping on something you spend a third of your life on.**

WATER

Every day I reach into my toolbox and grab my water bottle. I think most of us underestimate the importance of drinking water to stay healthy, even though we instinctively know that water is essential for healthy living. Doctors suggest women drink at least sixty-four ounces of water each day; men, 104, depending on exercise and weather. Of course, depending on your treatment, your doctor may advise you to drink more or less.

Sometimes drinking water all day can get a little boring, so I'll add a lemon or a little orange juice to keep it interesting. One of my clients going through treatment was told by her doctor to make sure she drank at least sixty-four ounces of water each day, and more on the days before and after chemo to help her recover quickly. She admitted to me it was a real struggle, especially because she wasn't used to having to track herself. I bought her a beautiful Nalgene bottle in her favorite color and had her get in the habit of drinking water with each meal, between each meal, and focus on drinking more on days before and after chemo.

She found it helped to change up the fruits and fruit juice she added to the water (she consulted with her doctor to find out which fruits to avoid with her treatment and medication). Within weeks she noted it was easier for her to recover from each chemo session, which gave her great incentive to continue her regime.

BREATHE

My next tool is deep breathing. We can't avoid all the stressors of life, especially during these difficult times, thus we need healthy ways to respond to them. **Deep breathing is an essential part of relaxation** because while you're focusing on taking slow, deep breaths you're not focusing on your stress.

YOGA

The day after I moved to Miami I started attending "Sunrise Beach Yoga" at 7 a.m. **Yoga helped to build my resilience, strength, balance, and flexibility.** Immersed in sunlight, sand, and salty air, I felt closer to my inner spirituality and emotionally stronger than I had in years.

I know, I know . . . you don't live near a beach, so why am I telling you this? I don't live near the beach anymore, either. However, I do have a TV with free yoga workouts that are awesome! Some even take place on the shoreline, so I'm at least there virtually. If you haven't tried yoga before, or you're too weak to stand, just start with Corpse Pose (Savasana). It's my favorite!

PRAYER

Prayer is another powerful tool for me. When I first awoke from my operation, I begged friends and family to pray with me "The Lord's Prayer." My solace lay in the phrase "Thy will be done." Those words helped me believe that I wasn't alone in fighting my war. **Having so many loved ones pray with and for me gave me the courage to keep fighting through my many battles.**

My wonderful brother would come to the hospital almost every day throughout my many stays and hold my hand and pray with me. When I didn't have the energy, he would pray aloud for the two of us. Many loved ones had masses said in my honor. My friends still hold my hand in church as we recite "The Lord's Prayer," fresh tears streaming down my cheeks with absolute gratitude for God and my army.

DIAPER

Another essential tool I travel with is a diaper. Yes, you read that correctly, an adult-sized diaper. With all my surgeries my body has been butchered, fileted, and put back together again. No surprise then to hear my body doesn't quite function properly. My nerves were damaged and although I'm lucky not to have to self-catheterize or use an ostomy for the rest of my life, I don't always know when I need to use the bathroom.

Rather than sit in my room anxious about having a mishap, I decided to use this new tool to get out and enjoy life. **I wear a diaper most days now and I don't have to worry about finding a bathroom when I'm in a car, at a concert, hiking, biking, or enjoying some other wonderful adventure.** (And yes, you can absolutely wear sexy underwear over one.) It's given me a freedom I never thought possible and I wish I had found this tool a long time ago.

EXERCISE GEAR

I love exercise gear that helps me stay active. My go-to is an electric bike (E-bike), a bicycle equipped with a motor to assist me when I'm pedaling. Depending on how my body is feeling, I'm able to enjoy biking on all terrains and use the motor to assist me as much as needed.

My sister, another cancer survivor, loves her E-bike as well. Because of the reassurance the engine provides, we've been able to push ourselves on our biking adventures. Even during the hot summer days, you'll see us cycling up the steepest of hills during our thirty-mile treks.

When I'm not using my E-bike, I'm using flippers to swim laps, stretch bands to gain flexibility, or a jump rope to build endurance. Use whatever works for you, just don't give up!

A MIRROR

It may seem surprising, but the mirror was another important tool in my arsenal. When you've worn the shoes of a cancer patient who is sick and tired of being an emaciated, bald victim of chemo, or a bloated, half-bald victim of steroids, it's okay to take a moment to be vain.

It is a gift to look in the mirror and see yourself healthy and thriving rather than disheveled and washed-out. It elicits hope, not just in you but in those who care about you too.

WIGS

When I first started packing my toolbox, I loaded in the two beautiful, albeit expensive wigs from my daughters' brilliant wig party. Unfortunately, they couldn't withstand the wear and tear of daily use. **I quickly realized I would be better served by inexpensive wigs that I could trim as my style and their split ends demanded.** It was a game-changer. Now I could have lots of fun new looks, from long blonde curls, medium straight brunette, to short redhead just to name a few.

I remember having a holiday dinner with my dear friend's family. My wig hadn't quite survived our morning hike, so after dinner I went upstairs to change styles. When I explained the new look, my friend's nephew asked if he could have the ruined hairpiece. Five days later my friend sent me a picture of her nephew adorned in my wig, skiing down a double-black-diamond, grinning ear to ear. Since then, I've sent him more cheap wigs which he has sported at weddings and other events. Seeing him rock that look made me realize I could handle losing my hair again if cancer returned.

Unfortunately, wigs didn't work for me after my brain surgery. Three days after the operation I got consent from my doctor to fly to D.C. and attend a wedding. I was elated until the nurse took off my bandages and handed me a mirror. I was furious with myself. Why had I agreed to go? With my forehead devoid of hair, the enormous scar across my face was visible and grotesque. I couldn't wear a wig since the webbing to hold it in place would tear into my stitches. What was I to do?

HAIR EXTENSIONS

As soon as I left the doctor's office, I called my wonderful friend. She has an answer for everything, and this time was no exception. "Too easy, Nancy. We're getting you hair extensions!"

I perked up, not knowing how hair-extensions would work given there was no hair in the front to attach anything to. "How? Where? When?" I sputtered.

"Oh, trust me," she said, her enthusiasm spilling out over the phone. "It's the same salon I took you to when you first started growing your hair back. I'll swing by to pick you up and take you there myself!"

My devoted hairdresser gave me the biggest hug when we arrived, shocked by the news of my brain tumor, and conferred with his colleague on how to get me back to looking my best. In a wild frenzy they grabbed strands of hair-extensions and deftly wove them to what little hair I still had. My back faced the mirror while they worked their magic and two hours later, they unveiled their masterpiece.

I stared at my beautifully coiffed long blond mane in the reflection. Was that really me? No one would ever guess I had just had surgery. **I looked at my reflection again and was nearly fooled myself. My half-bald head had been transformed.** I looked at my friend with tears in my eyes. My army had come to my rescue again. "Now," she said "We just have to get you healthy enough to walk on the plane by yourself."

AESTHETICIAN

As my hair and appearance started returning to normal, certain features were slower to heal than others. My short hair accentuated my face, revealing dull skin, aggressive lines, and wrinkles that made me look ten years older than I was. I was lucky to find an amazing aesthetician in Miami who helped me begin to look and feel healthier than I had in years. She was an integral part of my army and I am so grateful for her expertise and compassion.

When I moved back to Philadelphia, I returned to my aesthetician from my pre-cancer days. She too has been a soldier through this journey, being an incredible cheerleader for years. Slowly but surely, we have worked together to help my skin restore its collagen, smoothing the wrinkles and returning its natural glow.

When I look in the mirror now, I don't see a woman who survived cancer, I see a healthy person enjoying life. The two of us agree; when you look healthy, you act healthy and take better care of yourself in all facets.

ERASER

Although I use it sparingly, another tool I carry is an eraser. I use mine to remove toxic people from my life. **I realized the hard way that some of my worst stress came from people rather than circumstances.** In order to survive traumatic experiences, you must be wise enough to know what you need to heal and restore your well-being. Sadly, some people may not be capable of providing the sanctuary you truly need. Some go AWOL and some need to be discharged. This vital element of self-care offers you the opportunity to choose *yourself* and let them go.

PENCIL

With my eraser always comes a pencil, and I use this when considering a new relationship. First, ask yourself if you're honestly ready for a new relationship or if you are just trying to fill a void. Remember the adage "Put your oxygen mask on first" and take care of your needs before letting yourself care for someone else. It's important in *Becoming the Best U* to take the time you need to first heal yourself and create the life you want.

Once you're happy with yourself and your new life you can open the door to new relationships. Your pencil will come in handy now. That new person may be great for just one date or three, but if it doesn't feel right, know your eraser is always there for you.

BOXES AND PAINTBRUSH

In my toolbox, I also carry boxes and a paintbrush to give my space a new look when necessary. A few months after my remission I lost my marriage and my father. It was a very challenging time for me. My daughters were living in New York City, and I feared my emaciated body would not survive the winter. I felt a change would be healthy.

My bedroom revealed the chaos my heart was dealing with. It was time to start decluttering and organizing my space. I started getting rid of whatever reminded me of cancer and anyone who diminished my self-worth. I enlisted a good friend who understood my cancer and trauma to take on part of the emotional burden of ridding myself of memorabilia. She was a great advocate for keeping me accountable as I decided what to do with each object. It was extremely cathartic. I humbly suggest you try it even if you're currently in a healthy and positive state of mind.

Don't throw away all keepsakes as some things, say a lovely decorative platter or new wig you never wore, may be a great item to donate to a thrift store. If there's something of value, perhaps consider selling it. **Exorcise your demons one room at a time.** Let's say you decide to start in your bathroom. Set a timer for fifteen minutes. Pick a drawer and get started.

If you're finding it difficult to throw things out, that's normal. Fifteen minutes at a time of sorting your belongings can quickly add up to decluttering a whole room. The most important thing is to get started, be kind to yourself, and if you get frustrated remember every day is a new day and a good day to reset. If you find it challenging to stay organized or decluttered, call back your friend or call in the experts.

Once you've cleared your space, especially your bedroom, it's time to reach into your toolbox and pick up the paint brush. Depending on your taste and budget, **it can be easy to create a serene atmosphere that will help recharge you**. The first tip experts recommend is to be adventurous with color. If you're not feeling confident just paint one wall as an accent. Just changing your wall color can create a whole new environment.

The next tip is to add lighting to your space. Great lighting creates different moods and thus new energy in your home. If you're a DIY type, try different bulb wattages and change around your lamps. The only way you'll know what you like is by experimenting.

The third tip is to add plants to your space. If you don't have a green thumb, even fake plants have been shown to provide health benefits including reduced blood pressure and stress. If you're a stickler for the real thing, check online or with a nursery to find out which varieties are easiest to grow indoors. Not only do plants have a restorative quality, they help re-oxygenate their surroundings. You might choose a fragrant plant you love to place in your family area.

Most importantly, have fun. Enlist your partner or a family member for their help, but remember this is your peaceful retreat and a huge part of your healing process.

PERHAPS A MOVE?

Sometimes, however, no amount of redecorating will relieve the anxiety and fears. **I have known others who moved away after remission or another life challenge and seemed to appreciate a fresh new start. It certainly worked for me!**

The first day I moved into my Miami condo, I reached into my toolbox and picked up the paintbrush. I was adventurous with color, bought some fun mid-century modern furniture, added better lighting, and rushed out to buy some tropical plants and fresh herbs to grow on my balcony. It became my haven, a peaceful retreat, and a huge part of my healing process.

BUCKET LIST

Taped to the inside of my toolbox is a bucket list of future adventures. Everyone has dreams. What are yours? Perhaps you'd love to ride in a hot air balloon, swim with dolphins, peer over the edge of the Grand Canyon, or jump out of an airplane. I've been working through my bucket list for years and I'm always adding to it. Not all of my bucket list entries have been exotic excursions. This year part of my list read:

- Live to see my new grandson

- Live to see my daughter's med school white coat ceremony

- Be fit enough to be able to ski with my son, and

- Write this book

I am so blessed to have checked them off.

It's never too late to start writing your bucket list and tackling them one by one. Your dreams can be small or great. **Having something to look forward to makes it easier to keep fighting.**

I'm always turning around and finding another tool to get me through life's challenges. Each day brings new opportunities and with them new obstacles. Do you have a toolbox? If not, I recommend you get one and start packing. As George Herbert wisely counseled us, *"Do not wait; the time will never be 'just right.'"*

Reflections for the Warrior

- I learned I needed to pack a toolbox with many strategies and mindsets for life. Write a list of some of the tools you've packed.

    1.

    2.

    3.

- I learned I needed to be able to change my perspective to "glass half-full" when facing a tough situation. List a situation right now where you are willing to change your perspective for the better.

    _____

    _____

    _____

    _____

- I learned I needed to keep working on my bucket list. Write down something on your bucket list and how you might start achieving it today.

    _____

    _____

    _____

    _____

Please remember, just one idea can make a difference!

Musings from a Caregiver

Being a caregiver is all about adapting to changing circumstances. You'll never be prepared for everything your warrior's challenge can throw at you, but you can be ready to tackle whatever comes with a positive attitude. The most important thing in my toolbox is a sense of humor and optimism. Attitudes can be infectious, and happy people are healthier people.

You'll also find yourself taking totally impromptu trips to the hospital! So fun. Sometimes you may even get to sleep over! After a few attempts trying and failing to rest in a plastic upholstered chair armed only with the world's thinnest blanket and pillow combo, I decided to start bringing my own pillow and blanket. The first time a doctor had to wake me up was certainly a surprise, but a welcome one!

Also important is being able to entertain yourself while in a waiting room or doctor's office. Sure, we've all got tiny entertainment devices in our pockets all the time, but I always preferred having the option to share the time with my mom. Anything from a deck of cards to a joke book to a portable board game (I liked Hive and 7 Wonders Duels, but even just checkers or chess is great) will feel like a fulfilling way to spend your time and hopefully get your warrior's thoughts off any worries they may have.

Over time you'll learn more and more things that work for you and your situation, just remember to keep an eye out for tools and strategies that help make your caregiving journey easier and more fulfilling, and soon you'll be prepared for anything!

–Robert Rugart

Reflections for a Caregiver

- Everyone has different lessons to offer from their life. Write some tools you've developed that you think would help your warrior through this challenge.

    1.

    2.

    3.

- Changing your perspective can help you during this challenging time. Is there something bothering you right now? List one way to tackle the problem with a positive perspective.

    _____

    _____

    _____

    _____

- Ask your warrior about their bucket list. Write one thing the two of you could do together.

    _____

    _____

    _____

    _____

8

You'll Never Walk Alone

Grief is the price we pay for love.
–Queen Elizabeth II

I've had to deal with a roller coaster of emotions during my cancer journey, but I was never prepared for survivor's guilt. It was one of the main reasons I put off writing this book. How could I write about enduring cancer when I know that so many people reading this have either lost loved ones to cancer or would soon succumb themselves?

Throughout this marathon with cancer, I've been fortunate to tell my story to hundreds of people—in the waiting room at the doctor's office, in line at pharmacies, during sunrise yoga—people were always shocked to see me there at all, much less returning week after week. During each of these conversations, my story always got a similar response: "Oh my goodness, you need to write a book! How DID you do it?"

The answer, honestly, is I don't know. I don't know why I survived. I got lucky. But I know that I would have died without the lessons my caregivers taught me, and these are the lessons I needed to share.

So, how do I go about writing my story, much less an entire book?

My childhood friend gave me great advice. "Just start writing," she said in her gentle voice.

She's always been practical, and her advice made sense. Alright, I thought. I'll get started and see how I feel. She was right. Once the dam broke, words cascaded onto the page. Along the way I discovered that these lessons weren't just for my war with cancer; these were lessons for the rest of my life.

Everyone asked me how I was going to end this book, and again, I was daunted. I had no idea, just as I didn't know what I was supposed to write in the first place. So, when I was done writing chapter seven about packing a toolbox for life, I called my dear friend back and asked her what to do. She genuinely laughed into the phone and again said, "Just start writing."

I came home after having dinner out with some friends and was inspired to ask Alexa to play one of my father's favorite songs, "You'll Never Walk Alone," by Gerry and The Pacemakers. My dad had a beautiful bass voice and loved to serenade us whether we were in the kitchen doing dishes, driving to an exotic locale, or just sitting on the deck enjoying life. Tears started flowing. I really missed him! I sat down to write and asked Alexa to put the song on repeat, and through my tears of joy and grief, I wrote this last chapter without looking up.

Thanks, Dad, for your inspiration once again!

It was a beautiful, balmy August afternoon. My dad and I were sitting together, the two of us relaxing on patio chairs next to the koi pond I had built. It was a bittersweet moment watching the beautiful, ornamental fish as they jetted between water lilies. My dad insisted on visiting despite the fact that he was fighting cancer too.

He was a true warrior, having battled melanoma at forty-five, fifty-five, and sixty-five, breast cancer at sixty-three, prostate cancer at sixty and seventy-nine, bladder cancer at eighty-two, and now it looked like cancer was finally going to win. He was my hero. I never once heard him complain. No one did. Everyone who met him knew that, however dire the situation, when asked how he was doing he would always smile and say, "Fantastic!"

He actually meant it too.

My dad was an amazing father, and we always had a great relationship, but with five other siblings and his working full time we'd never forged that same special bond I had shared with my mom. The two of us battling cancer together changed everything. We were comrades in arms and we were both willing to do anything to help each other. During our cancer journey, we frequently talked about topics we had never discussed before, realizing we no longer had the luxury of time. We had been sitting together for what seemed like an hour, both of us too weary to talk, enjoying the peace of knowing what the other was going through. We were both staring death in the face, but I knew we were secretly hoping the other would give us permission to surrender first.

My father broke the silence, turning to me and taking my hand, "No parent wants to lose their child. There's no greater tragedy."

I looked at him, my heart breaking, seeing tears well up in his eyes. "I know," I answered, stifling the sobs, not wanting to accept what I already knew.

I lost my father the next year, months after my own remission. I was devastated. I had been fighting alongside him for what felt like an eternity and his death made my remission a Pyrrhic victory.

Although my move to Miami helped me heal, both physically and emotionally, I was painfully reminded just how lucky I had been to survive. Despite phenomenal medical care and a formidable army, I was only ever one mistake or misfortune from succumbing to this disease. My client from Philadelphia was battling her own cancer and needed a vacation. We made plans and set a date. When I called two days before to confirm, her son answered to share the devastating news that she had died the day before.

That same month I enrolled in real estate classes with an amazing professor who had just survived breast cancer. She became my mentor, and after the class I joined her brokerage firm. One day she called me to confide that her doctors recently discovered a brain tumor and surgery was scheduled three days hence. I promised to come visit the next day but unfortunately, she didn't have a fighting chance. Her sweet husband called me that morning to let me know she had died in her sleep.

Soon thereafter another dear friend called me. Through controlled sobs she shared that her daughter, who I had known and admired, had been killed in a car accident. Three years later, almost to the day, she shared more devastating news. In a cruel twist of fate, another car accident had taken her only other child. I flew to Philadelphia to see her. I had been thinking of her often, struggling to comprehend her grief and healing process. After we talked for a while, she said something that changed my life. "I try to live each day fully, the way my children would have wanted me to—to lead with kindness and a generous heart. Though I often grieve their loss, I try to remind myself that 'grief is the price we pay for love.'"

I know I often say life is not for the faint of heart. Even bolstered by my friend's inspiring words I still have trouble accepting life's cruelties. While writing this book, I lost my brother to sepsis after a routine shoulder surgery. The tragic irony is that he had said his goodbyes to me when I was suffering with cancer but, because he died so suddenly, I never had a chance to say goodbye to him. No one did, not even his beloved wife or children. It wasn't until my siblings and I were standing together holding hands in front of his casket that we viscerally felt his loss. Because of his death I feel a stronger bond now with my siblings than I ever have. Why must we suffer tragic loss to recognize our deepest love?

Life is full of tragedies and they're never fair. It doesn't matter if we're young or old, black or white, rich or poor. Tragedies burn down your world. It's up to you whether you give up or find a way to make a new life with what you've recovered from the ashes. There have been many times I've asked "why me?" Why did I get cancer when so many did not? Why have I survived when so many did not? Maybe there is no answer.

Now that I'm living back in Philadelphia and am still in remission, I realize I've been asking the wrong question. Instead of asking "why me," I should have been asking "how can I help others like me?" I've donated, participated in studies, walked 5Ks for the cure, still it hasn't been enough.

We wrote this book to let others know they are not alone. Cancer isn't just dealing with surgeries, chemo, and radiation. It's living with an ostomy that might leak feces all over your new outfit, having clumps of your hair fall out in the shower, and flirting with bankruptcy while fighting for insurance to pay their share. It's waking up in an upside-down world, trying to find a way to make it to the next day, and coming to terms with your new normal.

Whether you're a warrior or a caregiver, when your goal in life is to leave a legacy of love, the story of your days will be one of kindness. The more prepared we are for life's challenges the better our perspective, confidence, and fortitude will be.

I've learned that when we have the courage to change the things we can, ask for help, get our affairs in order, push ourselves, take life one step at a time, pack a toolbox of strategies, and accept that grief is the price we pay for love, we become more resilient, optimistic, and able to transform our lives.

No journey will be the same, so please be gentle with yourself. And although there will be more unforeseeable obstacles ahead, remember that what you have lost and learned is key to becoming the best U–Upbeat, Unstoppable, and Unafraid.

A Caregiver's Parting Thoughts

We were lucky that my mom's journey went as well as it did. I would love to write here that she beat cancer and never looked back, but in reality, the fight took its toll and every extra day with her is a blessing. Many, like my granddad, weren't as fortunate. The natural response is to ask yourself what you did wrong, but I implore you to instead celebrate what you did right. Recall moments when you brought a smile to your loved one's face, or they yours. It's okay to feel grief. Don't avoid it, rather embrace it. Let it help you cherish and celebrate their memory.

Sometimes the war ends with both sides fighting to their last breath, other times one side realizes that surrendering is what is best for their army in the long run. Don't hold it against your warrior if that is the path they choose, but don't let them choose it lightly either. For many near the end of life, a peaceful month is worth more than a war-torn year.

At the end of the day, it's your warrior's journey. Just be glad you could share it with them, and when grief inevitably strikes, remember that it's just the price we pay for love.

Letter to Our Readers

Dear Reader,

Thank you for spending your precious time reading our book. Our mission is to help patients, caregivers, and survivors navigate the unchartered waters of cancer and make their path a little more peaceful, optimistic, fun, and empowered. We don't expect you to love every chapter or agree with everything we did to get through my cancer journey. As I've said, no journey will be the same.

What we're hoping is that there is one thing you take from this book, whether you're moved by something my caregivers did, or you feel empowered to ask others for help, or you are inspired to reach out to a loved one and offer your support. Whatever you've gleaned, we'd love to hear from you! Let us know how we helped you in *Becoming the Best U*—Upbeat, Unstoppable, and Unafraid!

Robert and I are available for speaking, coaching, seminars, and engagements. Just as importantly, we'd love to hear about your cancer journey and what lessons cancer taught you and your caregivers! For further information, check out our website BecomingTheBestU.com or email us directly at info@becomingthebestu.com.

Thank you again for being part of a wonderful and supportive member of our cancer community!

If you'd like to follow us for more—

Facebook: BecomingtheBestU
Instagram: UpbeatUnstoppableUnafraid.

Kindly,
Nancy & Robert

About the Authors

Nancy is the founder of Becoming the Best U and a survivor of stage 4 ovarian cancer and metastatic brain cancer. As a wellness and relationship coach, author, and columnist, she helps men and women navigate life's challenges to become Upbeat, Unstoppable, and Unafraid through one-on-one coaching, group seminars, and as a guest speaker. She has been an award-winning documentary filmmaker, a PBS on-air personality, and earned her Masters of Education. She loves rock climbing, spending time with her grandson, and going on bike rides with friends and family.

Robert is the co-founder of Becoming the Best U. He left his job in finance to help write this book and inspire and empower caregivers based on his own experience caregiving for his mom, grandfather, and wife. During Nancy's cancer journey, Robert shared his gifts of playing piano and singing, making theirs the most popular floor in the hospital. He has sung professionally, directed an award-winning documentary, and earned his Masters of Chemical Engineering. He loves entertaining his nephew, skiing with friends and family, and singing in his a cappella group.

www.ingramcontent.com/pod-product-compliance
Lightning Source LLC
Chambersburg PA
CBHW060333130626
46553CB00003B/999

* 9 7 9 8 9 8 9 1 2 5 0 0 5 *